Beautiful
New Mexico

Gila National Forest

Beautiful
New Mexico

Concept and Design: Robert D. Shangle
Text: Craig Ryan

First Printing September, 1979
Published by Beautiful America Publishing Company
P.O. Box 608, Beaverton, Oregon 97075
Robert D. Shangle, Publisher

Library of Congress Cataloging in Publication Data
Beautiful New Mexico
Ryan, Craig, 1953-
1. New Mexico—Description and travel—1951—Views. I. Title
F797.R9   917.89   79-16748
ISBN 0-89802-073-5
ISBN 0-89802-072-7 (pbk.)

Copyright © 1979 by Beautiful America Publishing Company
Printed in the United States of America

Photo Credits

GENE AHRENS—*page, 33, page 35.*

ROY BISHOP—*page 8.*

LIONEL AND CAROL BROWN—*page 2; page 11; pages 12-13; page 18; page 23; page 27; pages 28-29; page 39; page 34; page 35; pages 36-37; page 38; page 42; page 43; page 46; page 54; page 58; page 59; page 62; page 63; page 66; page 70; page 71; page 75.*

WILLARD CLAY—*page 47; page 50; page 55; page 76.*

BOB CLEMENZ—*pages 20-21.*

ED COOPER—*page 6.*

ROBERT SHANGLE—*page 31; page 39; page 65; page 68; page 73; page 78; page 80.*

JERRY SIEVE—*page 14; page 17; page 24; page 40; page 44; page 49; pages 52-53; page 56; pages 60-61; page 69; page 72.*

Beautiful America Publishing Company
The nation's foremost publisher of quality color photography

Current Books

Alaska, Arizona, British Columbia, California, California Vol. II, California Coast, California Desert, California Missions, Colorado, Florida, Georgia, Hawaii, Los Angeles, Idaho, Illinois, Maryland, Michigan, Michigan Vol. II, Minnesota, Montana, Montana Vol. II, Mt. Hood (Oregon), New York, New Mexico, Northern California, Northern California Vol. II, North Idaho, Oregon, Oregon Vol. II, Oregon Coast, Oregon Mountains, Portland, Pennsylvania, San Diego, San Francisco, Texas, Utah, Virginia, Washington, Washington Vol. II, Washington D.C., Wisconsin, Yosemite National Park

Forthcoming Books

California Mountains, Indiana, Kentucky, Las Vegas, Massachusetts, Mississippi, Missouri, Nevada, New Jersey, North Carolina, Oklahoma, Ozarks, Rocky Mountains, San Juan Islands, Seattle, South Carolina, Tennessee, Vermont, Wyoming

Large Format, Hardbound Books

Beautiful America, Beauty of California, Glory of Nature's Form, Lewis & Clark Country, Western Impressions

Lithography by Fremont Litho Inc., Fremont, California

Contents

Introduction..7

Southeast—
　Tularosa Basin to the Staked Plains......................16

Northeast—
　Wilds of Cimarron to the Great Grasslands................25

Northwest—
　Navajo Land to the Mesas of Acoma........................41

Southwest—
　Gila Wilderness to the Rio Grande........................57

North-Central—
　Pueblo Heartland and the Historic Cradle.................74

Enlarged Prints

Most of the photography in this book is available as photographic enlargements. Send self-addressed, stamped envelope for information. For a complete product catalog, send $1.00.
Beautiful America Publishing Company
P.O. Box 608
Beaverton, Oregon 97075

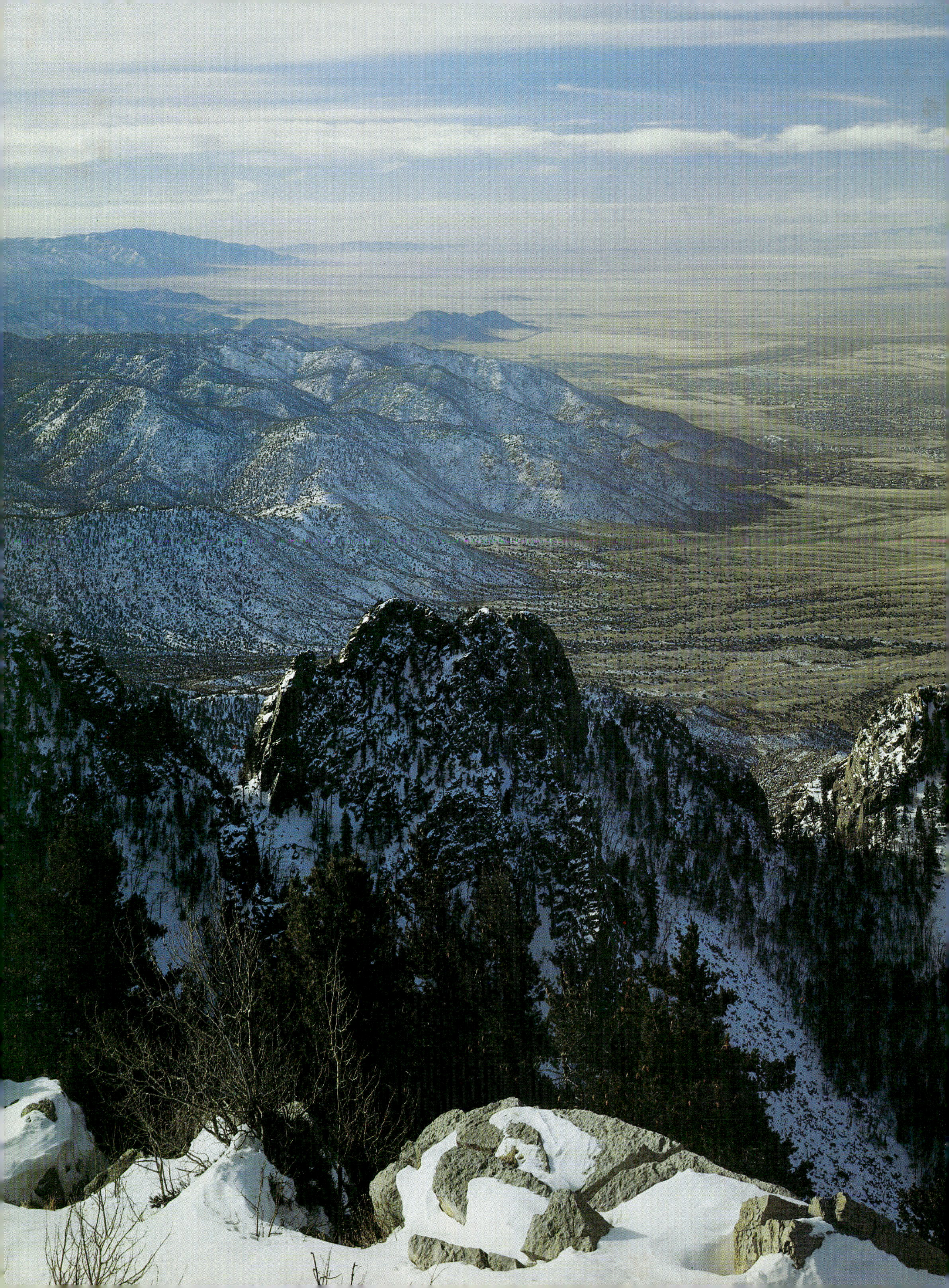

Introduction

The notion that you need a passport to visit New Mexico may raise a smile these days. But until fairly recently, New Mexico might as well have been a foreign country for all the attention it got from residents of the other 49. Even the folks who knew precisely where it was usually didn't have much idea what could be found there: the mysterious mesas, scorched deserts and fir-covered peaks of the 47th state were known primarily to those lucky Americans privileged to call themselves New Mexicans.

Indeed, New Mexico has the mystique of a foreign land: environmentally, historically and culturally it is unique. Here in the heart of the southwestern United States is a sun-drenched spread of vast, open spaces and immense silences, awesome granite spires and sandstone canyons, wild and remote deserts. People of Spanish, American Indian and Anglo descent have lived side by side for centuries—though not always amiably—and they have managed to forge a rich and rewarding existence from the raw stuff of New Mexico.

While the idea of New Mexico may seem new to most Americans, the state is old in terms of length of human habitation. There were men here 25,000 years ago, the earliest civilization in North America; and there have been men here ever since. Some have left their marks on the land. Cliff dwellings, pueblos, mine shafts and ghost towns all remain to show how New Mexicans lived in the recent or the far-distant past.

Today's New Mexican, unlike his Indian, Spanish or Anglo ancestors, is careful not to leave his mark on the land: the residents of this ''land of enchantment'' are scrupulous caretakers of their homeland. Lakes and mountains sacred to the Pueblo and Navajo have been protected from the inroads of technological society. Mines that scar the earth and mills that foul the air have been actively discouraged. Today's attitude is one of fierce pride and preservation; and the rest of the country owes the New Mexican a nod of gratitude for that.

New Mexico's diversity is nothing short of astounding. The blend of culture and landscape seems to contain everything. There are 73 separate mountain ranges

Sandia Mountains and Sandia Desert

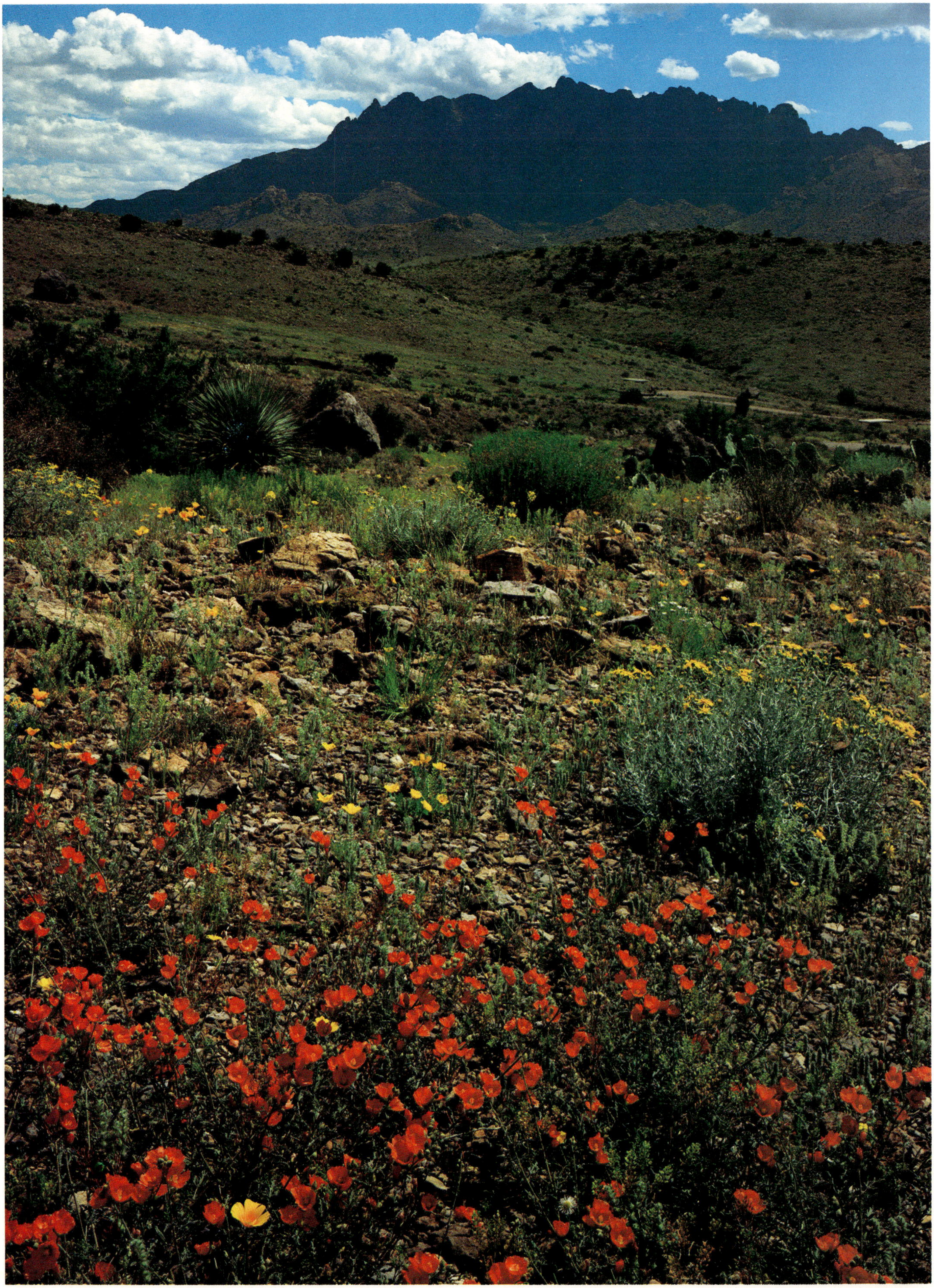

within this state's borders and hardly a spot on its soil from which mountains are not visible. They include the dense outcrops of alpine forest in the North as well as the desolate, sun-painted crags of the Southwest. There are rushing rivers cold enough to numb fingers, and splendid, unspoiled lakes. The boundless plains and grasslands of the East roll out like a becalmed ocean for countless miles.

The extremes are myriad. The searing fires of the desert sun contradict the sub-zero snow banks of the heights; dramatic stone towers rear hundreds of feet above the sleepy prairies; the arid silence of a summer's afternoon is shattered by the sudden lash of a thunderstorm racing over the flatlands; the gleaming steel and glass of downtown Albuquerque nestles against the slumbering backdrop of the Sandia Mountains. Seven of the earth's eight life/climate zones are represented in New Mexico, illustrating the weather variations that exist.

Two factors common to the entire state are altitude and sun: even the very lowest plot of land sits at nearly 3,000 feet (with some mountain crests pushing above 13,000) and every square mile receives sunshine at least 70 per cent of the time, year round. This accounts, in part, for the refreshing New Mexico air: clear, clean and unexpectedly exhilarating. It may well be the freshest in the country. Consequently, it's hardly surprising to find that New Mexico welcomes throngs of visitors each season of the year. The Tourist Division of the state government boasts that whatever you like, and whenever you come, chances are good you'll find it here.

The history and people of the state make for a fascinating saga. Ancestors of the Pueblo Indians occupied the cliffs and mesas about 5,000 years ago. Without explanation they disappeared, leaving but few clues for the archaeologist. The later Pueblo groups thrived for centuries in the north-central portions, developing peaceful societies and raising their complex apartment cities from the rock. Navajos, Apaches and other nomadic tribes arrived later. The Spanish came north from their successful conquest of Mexico in the 16th century searching for the fabled "Seven Cities of Cibola," and hoping to establish missions among the Pueblos. And, in the 19th century, the first Anglo-Americans rode in from the east, eager to expand their infant nation and more than a little interested in the deposits of precious minerals, beaver pelts and the establishment of trade with Santa Fe. Today each of these elements co-mingle, endowing New Mexico with a cultural atmosphere unsurpassed in tradition and contrast.

The wildlife of the state is predictably varied and plentiful. The flora and fauna of the high desert mountains are unusually arresting. Bird sanctuaries boast species found nowhere else. Elk, bear and even antelope may be seen in their natural habitat. The cut-throat trout is the state fish and everywhere the lakes and streams tempt the fisherman with high sport and—assuming success—with indisputably delicious eating. And while it is true that several species of wildlife, once abundant, have through the centuries disappeared, it is a testament to the latter-day New Mexican's protective vigilance that many of these animals have not only been re-introduced but are, in some cases, flourishing once again.

New Mexico may be divided into five geographic regions, each region possessing a particular style and personality. The first and largest of these regions is the *Southeast.* The dominating features are the Sacramento and Guadalupe Mountains, the massive Tularosa basin, the sobering flatlands of the East and, of course, Carlsbad Caverns. Focal points of the *Northeast* are the historic Raton Pass and Santa Fe Trail, the Kiowa Grasslands, Cimarron Canyon and the perfect cone of Capulin Mountain. The Indian country of *Northwestern* New Mexico includes the extensive reaches of the Navajo Reservation, El Morro National Monument and the "Sky City" of Acoma. The remote *Southwest* region encompasses the bounteous Rio Grande Valley, the Gila Wilderness and the mineral-laden mountains with their ghost towns and barren desertscapes. The heart of New Mexico lies in the *North-Central* region and includes some famous cities and towns like Santa Fe (the capital), Taos (the artistic center), and Albuquerque (the largest). Other features are numerous pueblos, a volcanic caldera and the magnificent, snow-capped crests of the Sangre de Cristo Range.

Obviously, a book of this size cannot begin to explore the great wealth of New Mexico's beauty. All that is hoped is that the photographs and commentary which follow can contribute to an already formidable mosaic filling the New Mexican with pride, the traveler with a longing to return, and the faraway stranger with unabashed jealousy.

Aside from all the tangible things that can be cited in New Mexico's favor, there are some elusive feelings that haunt the visitor from the time he arrives until long after his departure: something he can take home with him to ponder. One of them is a sense of wonderment: "things just seem to look better in New Mexico than they do anywhere else." There's a sparkle, a liveliness, a clarity that is somehow pervasive here in a way that no other place can match. And that is not just travel-brochure exaggeration—some of the nation's renowned artists have noticed the same thing, and it is not without reason that many of them are now New Mexicans.

It is, of course, the inexplicable that men labor hardest to explain. We tend to think that explaining something is the same as understanding it; and some delicate phenomenon that defies our words will buzz incessantly in our minds like a single mosquito in our bedchamber. Actually, two things suggest themselves readily, and

Soapweed Yucca, New Mexico state flower
(Following pages) Shiprock in northwestern New Mexico

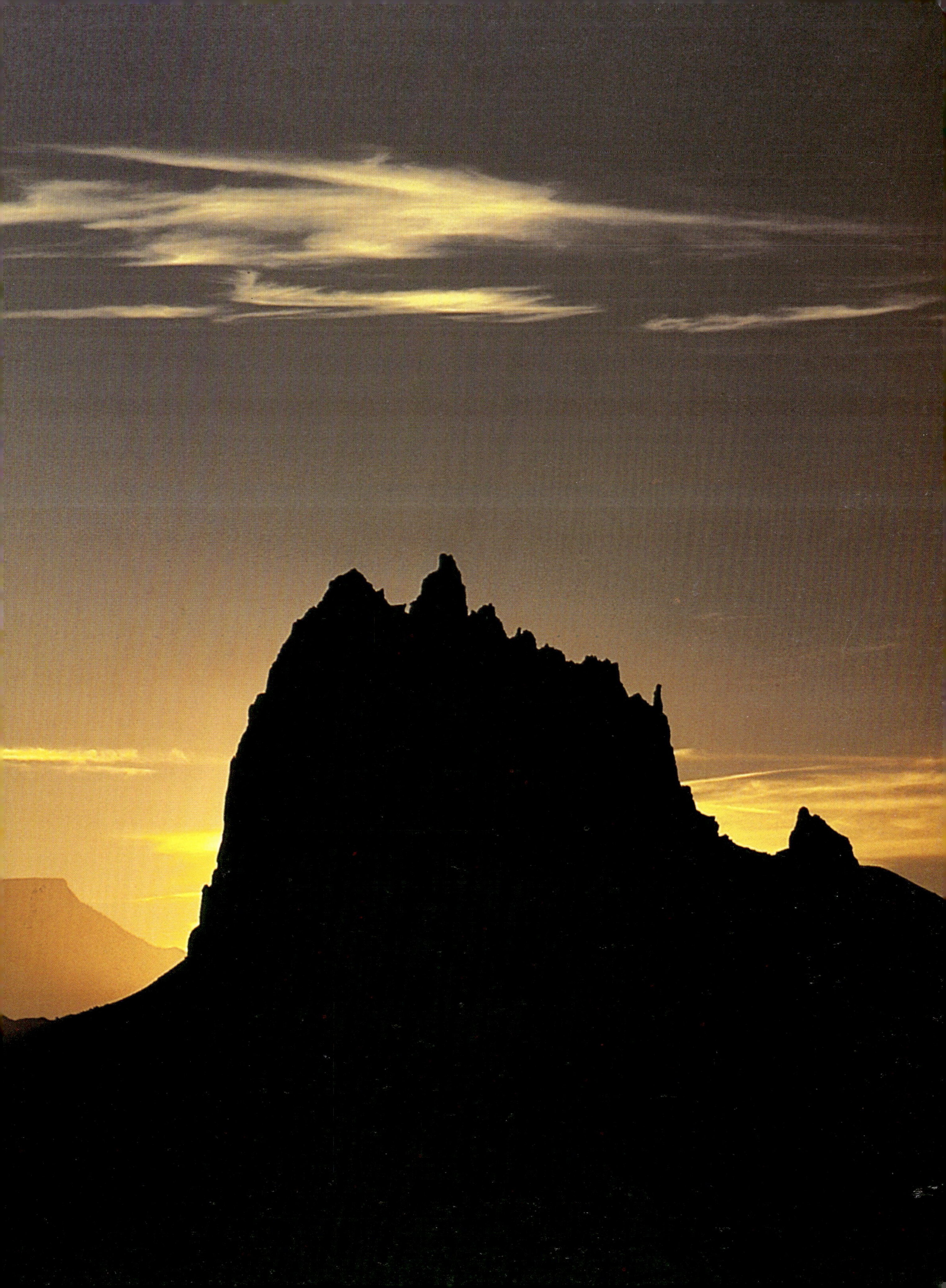

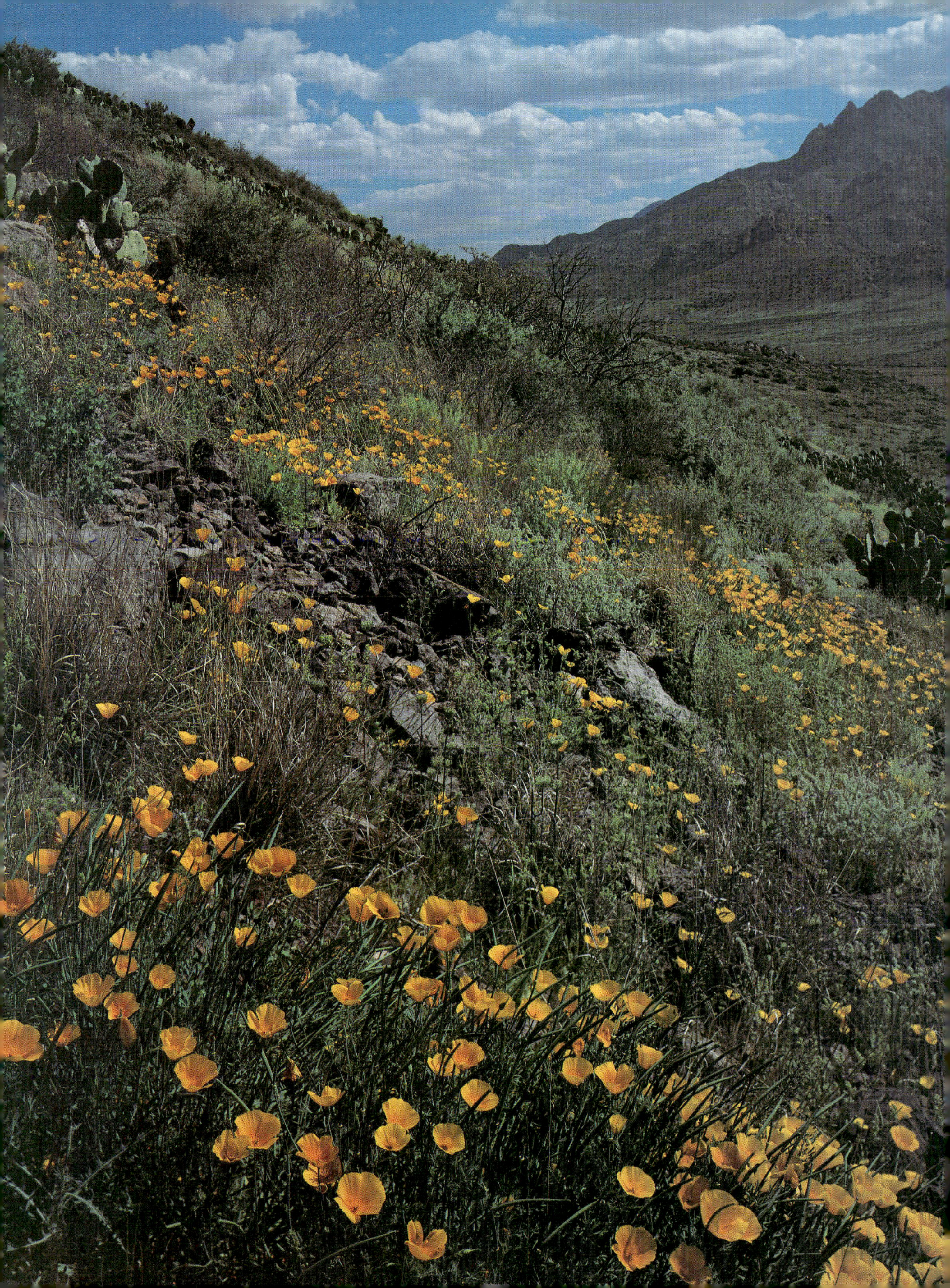

with problems like this it seems fitting to examine the simplest solutions first. One reason things look so good in New Mexico just might be the air: you can't see it. Instead of veiling distant objects in subtle haze or smog, or putting a ring of light brown around the edges of nature's blue dome, New Mexico's air draws attention to itself by not looking like much at all. So instead of looking at the air, you're looking at everything else, which seems to shine with an unaccustomed intensity in the absence of interference.

Well, that's one possible answer, and it's the simpler one. The second is . . . well, *enchantment.* Admittedly, magic is out of style right now, and sorcery is only something that used to be done a long time ago. In our modern age, as I said, we like to have explanations for things. We might even go so far as to say that things we can't explain rationally probably don't exist, though to claim something like that is to climb far out on a philosophical limb. Are we, after all, to claim that New Mexico probably isn't enchanting just because we don't know for sure what enchantment is? Let's answer it by begging the question: enchantment is what you feel when you visit New Mexico.

There's one other aspect of the state worth mentioning because it seems so nearly intangible: there is a "goodness of fit" in this state between man and his artifacts and the land. Somehow the cities do not impose on the landscape; ranches and irrigated farmlands complement the mountains and deserts without submerging them; even the most isolated and vulnerable of man's outposts seem to be in tune with their natural surroundings. The effect is somehow harmonious, and like good harmony anywhere, there is an almost restful feeling of rightness about it.

But the reason that man's artifacts seem in tune with nature is that in New Mexico, it is nature that calls the tune. This has never been an easy land to live in: the resources by which man lives are ever in short supply—especially the most important, water. Once a teacher spoke of the wisdom of the lilies of the field; the New Mexican, for survival, had rather pattern himself on the flowers of the desert, which can make a little water go a long way. Extremes of climate, ruggedness of terrain, and the demands of self-sufficiency have in this area, at least, formed a race of people who live closer to the land than most. And through greater closeness, they have developed greater appreciation.

More than anything else, the essence of New Mexico is the vigorous (often violent) blending and clashing of landscapes and people. The forces of nature rage gloriously unhampered here, and offer man, if he is of a character sufficiently tough and inventive, a raw beauty unequalled in stature and diversity anywhere in the world. And luckily, it can all be had without a passport.

Southeast—Tularosa Basin to the Staked Plains

When the first Spanish explorers entered New Mexico about 400 years ago, the dry desertlands of the Southeast stretched out before them like a bleached and uncharted sea. Coronado was the first European to lay eyes on this bone-dry prairie, for centuries home only to the Plains Indians and the peculiar hump-backed shaggies that came to be called buffalo. There were no landmarks to speak of, only the yucca and catclaw and the wind. That Spanish expedition passed through disappointed—they were looking for gold. But today this is prosperous cowboy country called the Staked Plains, or Llano Estacado, and the gold is the black kind—oil. No one has been able to do much about the heat, but the Staked Plains have become a flatbed of riches: cattle ranches, a steady flow of petrochemicals and the bounty of irrigated fields. Some have suggested that this treeless plane of earth is the single most level stretch of ground its size in the world.

For decades tourists have come in increasing numbers, most of them travelling US 285. Their destination is Carlsbad Caverns National Park, the undisputed granddaddy of caves. The town of Carlsbad sits on the banks of the Pecos River and is a jumping-off spot for a variety of adventures. In Carlsbad proper is the Living Desert State Park, a zoological-botanical complex offering an unrivaled potpourri of desert life for close observation. President's Park is here also: imagine a turn-of-the-century amusement park with vintage rides.

But the real attraction is the big cave. South of town the road slices through cactus-covered hillocks and winds up to the entrance of a cave explorer's fantasy world. Limestone caverns, containing more than 60 separate rooms, funnel down 750 feet beneath the desert floor. A three-mile hike takes you to the bottom, curling through the natural maze of tunnels framed by eerie deposits of dripping limestone

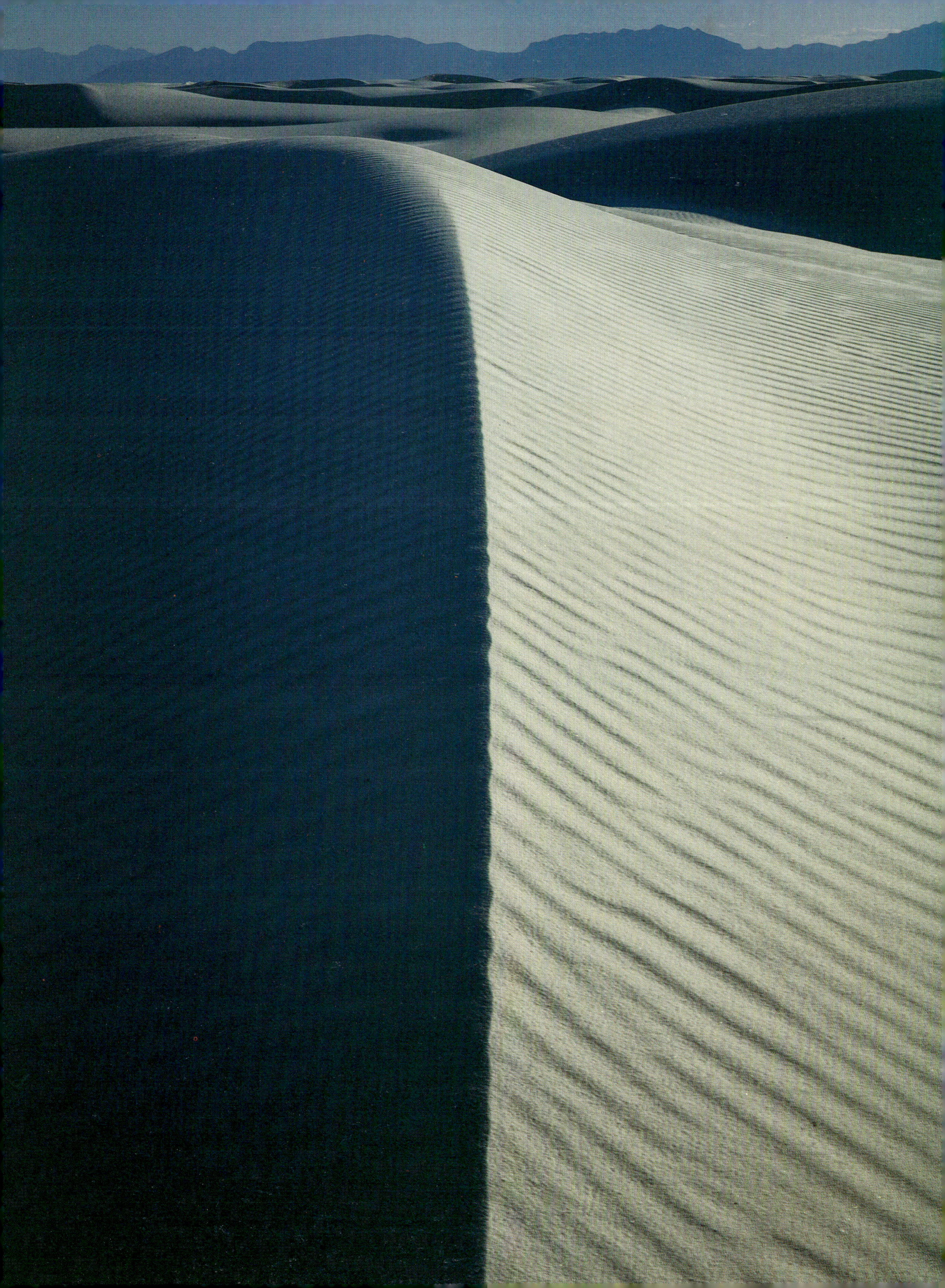

Hopewell Lake in the Brazos Mountains

(stalagmites and stalactites) which jut like marble daggers from every conceivable cranny. And don't worry about the walk back up: an elevator returns you to the top in a matter of seconds. It's an experience that leaves strong impressions: Iceberg Peak and Green Lake are down there, also the Big Room at the bottom. Its ceilings are 350 feet high.

West of Carlsbad is mountain country, and a modest blacktop road rolls into the Guadalupe Mountains clear to spectacular Sitting Bull Falls. These peaks and canyons were once a coral reef encircling an ancient inland sea. And there are more caverns inside this 100-mile range in the Lincoln National Forest, along with wild turkey, elk, black bear and mountain lion. For the hearty there are hiking trails through the gnarled canyons where rustlers, thieves and assorted bandits hid in the shade of the caves from the long arm of frontier law.

The Guadalupes gradually give way to the Sacramento chain and the rest of the national forest. Here in Apache country the summers are cool and the winters thick with snow. Approached from Artesia, on the Pecos, it's a jaunt of about 70 miles. The highway leads from the plains to Cloudcroft, high in the mountains. The view is superb and so is the skiing. A solar observatory is maintained at Sunspot (9,250 feet above sea level), a few miles south by a paved road skirting the crests. Excellent Forest Service trails offer a jumble of opportunities for the backpacker and horseman in the canyons below.

Due north of Cloudcroft, the mountains become the Mescalero Apache Indian Reservation, some 460,000 acres of spectacular forest. The Mescalero, successful ranchers and loggers, are justifiably proud of their well-managed mountainlands and streams. The wilderness is pristine, a sportsman's paradise. The powerful peaks of Sierra Blanca, sacred to the Mescalero, strain above 12,000 feet.

Just north of the reservation lies Ruidoso, site of the world's richest horse race at Ruidoso Downs each Labor Day. Ruidoso also hosts the annual Mescalero festival where the visitor can witness the spectacle of the Devil Dance, as well as the traditional all-Indian baseball game. Highway 37 runs up to Bonita and Nogal Lakes nestled in the lush forests of blackjack pine.

This is part of New Mexico's notorious Lincoln County, known to Western Americana buffs as the site of the Lincoln County range wars. To the east are the Capitan Mountains, to the north, the Jicarillas. But Lincoln itself, now a ghost town, is the place to start. Lincoln Town grew up along the banks of the Rio Bonito. This was the stomping ground of Billy the Kid, perhaps the most celebrated outlaw of the Old West. Still standing is the County Courthouse where the Kid, positioned in a

(Following pages) Taos Pueblo, Taos, New Mexico

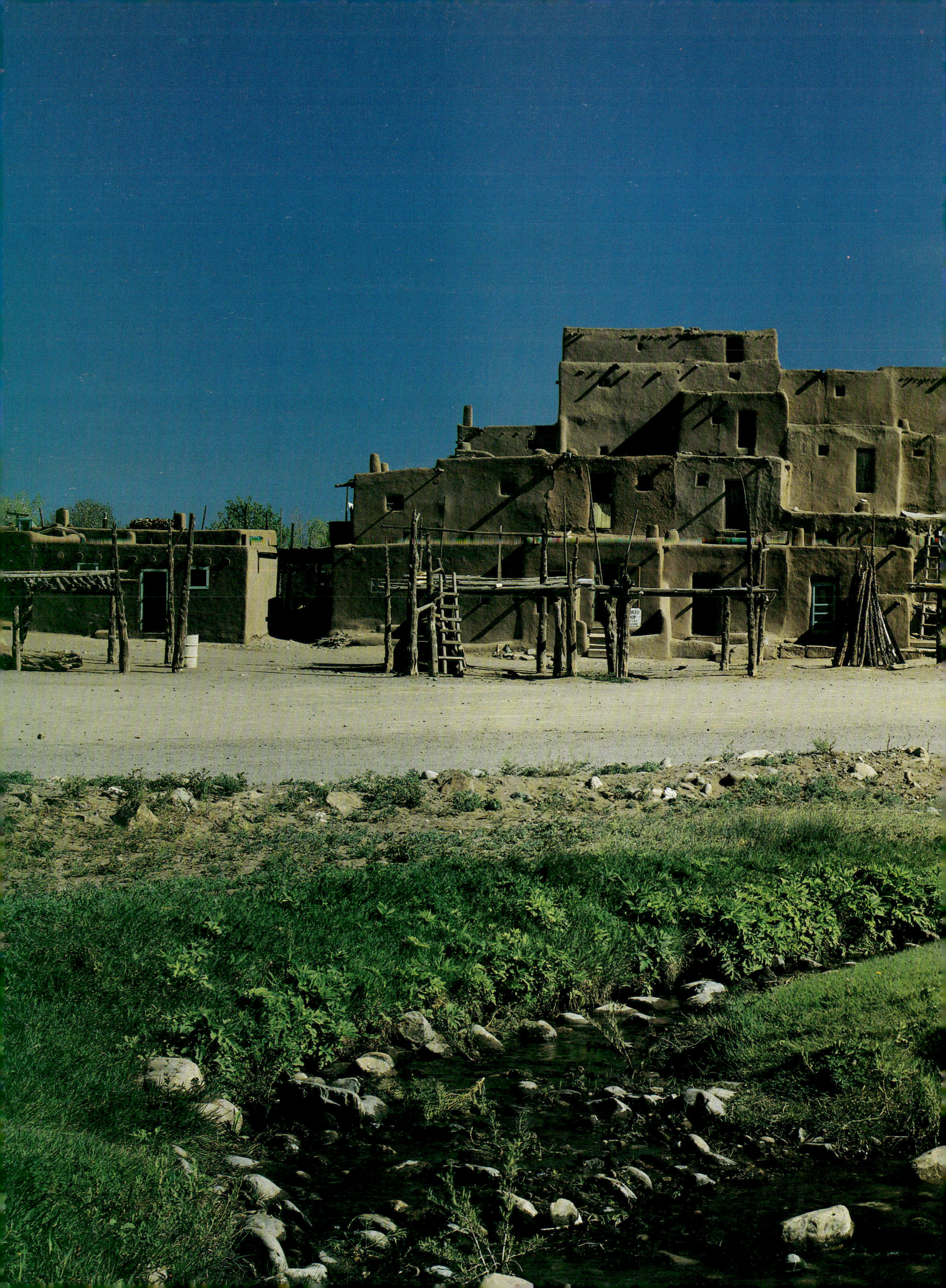

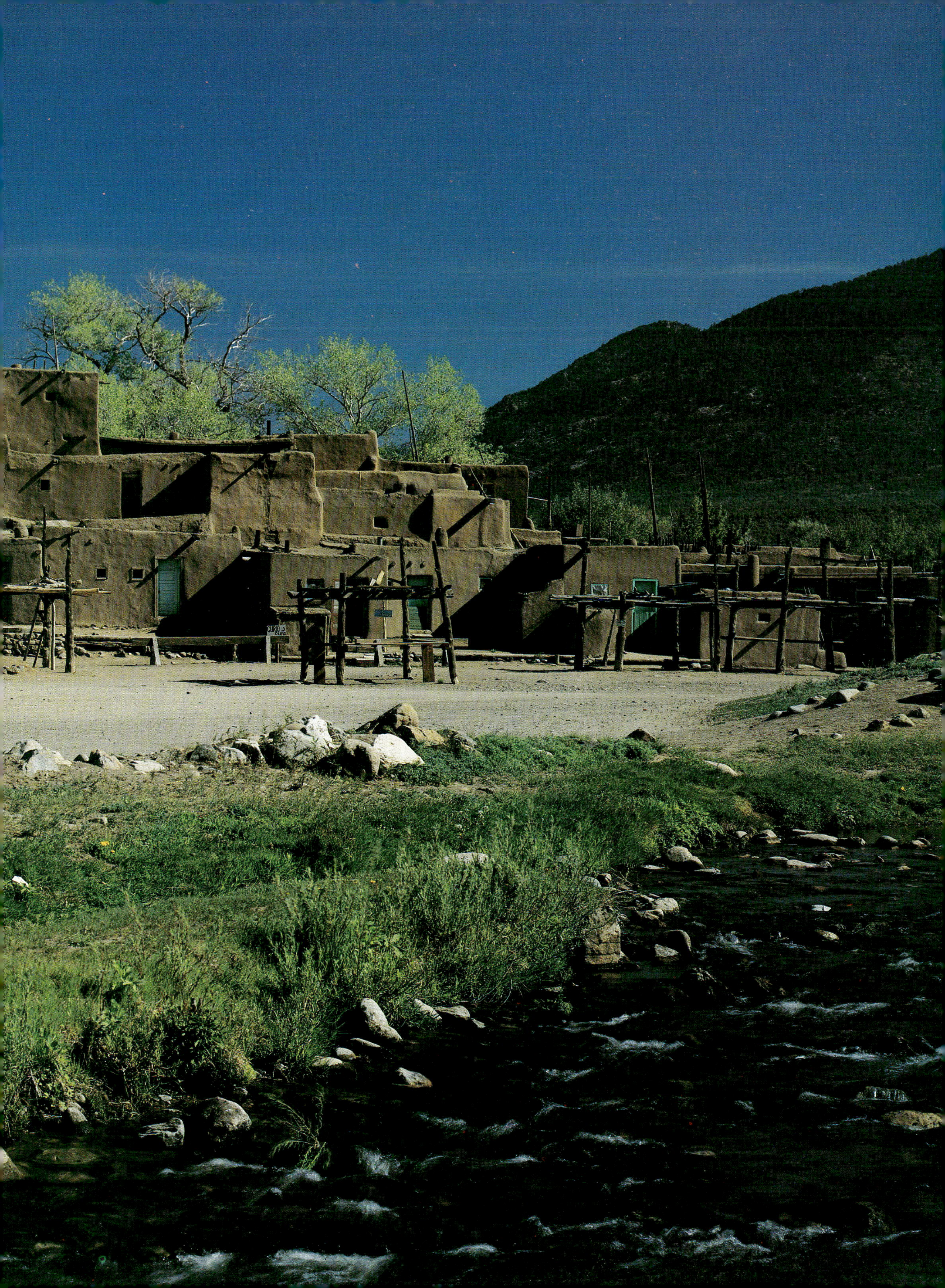

second-story window, killed Deputy Bob Olinger with a shotgun and, after shaking hands with local admirers, rode off into the proverbial sunset.

To the west of this mountain chain lies the sparse landscape of the Tularosa Basin. It's a 16-mile drive from Cloudcroft down to Alamagordo, the principal town in the parched valley below. Highway 82 descends through a mountain forest of spruce, aspen and pine to the creosote bushes, yucca plants and cottonwoods of the valley floor.

The Tularosa Basin is an immense depression bounded by the remote, uninhabited ridges of the San Andres Mountains on the western edge. Fifteen miles from Alamagordo, in the floor of the basin, sworls and dunes of shimmering crystals appear mirage-like beyond a rise: the White Sands National Monument. This cheery playground of the desert, with its softly crumbled masses of flowing gypsum, will attract more than a moment's glance and a few snapshots. Fierce rains and snowmelt carry tons of fine gypsum sand eroded from the San Andres into the natural basin below, creating a giant sandbox where dunes pile 50 feet high. This is the largest such deposit on earth. It's soft and pliable and looks like blown snow—and there's 275 square miles of it.

At first it's a surprise to find that life is so abundant here. More than 100 species of plant life spring from the constantly shifting white tides. Yuccas shoot from the sand to bloom in the sun, along with sumac, squawbush, rabbit brush and cottonwood trees. In addition to badgers, foxes and coyotes, rare animals like the bleached earless lizard also thrive here.

North from Alamagordo, through the town of Tularosa, US 54 joins the northern portions of the great basin and the Malpais: the Valley of Fires. Here is a 40-mile flow of black lava thought to be the longest of its kind in the country. Seventy feet thick in some spots, the Malpais is the essence of tortured desolation. The Chupadera Mesa lies to the north and beyond it the national monument at Gran Quivira, where, in the desert's harshest environs, Spanish priests and Pueblo Indians erected churches, tilled the earth and struggled valiantly against the odds to establish a life for their people. But the realities of the desert, severe drought and constant attacks by the Plains Indians, crushed their dreams. The Saline Pueblos, glorious monuments to their efforts, remain standing where men could no longer endure.

New Mexico windmill

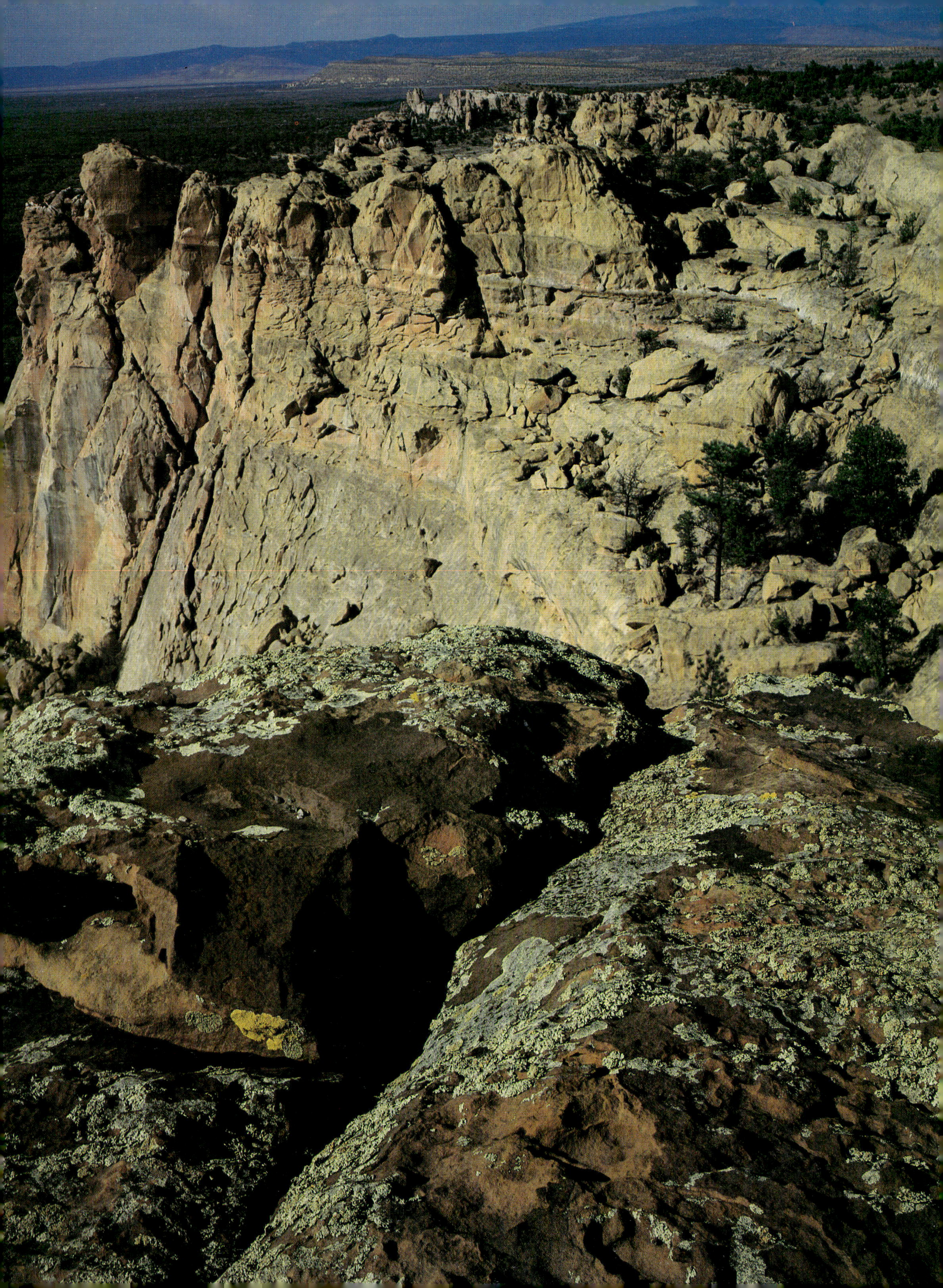

Northeast—
Wilds of Cimarron to the Great Grasslands

The western-bound American pioneers of the 19th century were faced with a dilemma when they reached the frontier of New Mexico on their way to Santa Fe. They had a choice of routes. They could approach from Colorado and head south through Raton Pass; a long and difficult journey. The steep windswept mountains and chilly temperatures made traveling slow. Yet the alternate course was scary enough to make the hardships of Raton seem welcome. The Cimarron Cutoff of the Santa Fe Trail enters New Mexico from what is now the Oklahoma panhandle, at first glance the ideal path to Fort Union and Santa Fe. The distance is shorter, the terrain relatively flat. Nevertheless, scarcity of water and danger of Indian attack made this short-cut a risky venture at best.

Today, the plains of northeastern New Mexico, characterized by tranquil grasslands and mountain cones standing isolated against the sky, are peaceful and content. Clayton is the first town inside the border, if you come in on the route of the old Cimarron Cutoff. The initial landmark, and one that signalled the beginning of the final stretch for the frontiersman, is Rabbit Ear Mountain. Like nearly all the mountains in northeast New Mexico, this one was once a great volcanic oven. The name derives from the Kiowa chief, Rabbit Ears, whose grave lies below.

The 40-mile expanse of wide-open grassy plains north and south of Clayton are part of the Kiowa National Grasslands, vestiges of the sea grass that blanketed much of the Western United States in prehistoric times. The remainder of the grasslands surround the town of Mills in the center of the Northeast region.

A short distance west and north of Clayton, the massive bulk of Sierra Grande (8,720 feet) stands on the horizon. And not far beyond, the astounding Capulin Mountain. Set aside as a national monument in 1916, Capulin is a volcanic

Sandstone Bluffs on Mt. Taylor

cindercone of near geometric perfection. A great circle at its base, the chokebberry-covered slopes rush evenly upward to the summit. A road spirals three miles up to the rim where a trail leads to the depths of Capulin's crater more than 400 feet below. The view of the surrounding country from the rim commands Sierra Grande and Laughlin Peak to the south, Rabbit Ear Mountain back to the east, and in the western distance, the magnificent Sangre de Cristo Range.

A few miles north of Capulin is the small town of Folsom. The first traces of what came to be called Folsom Man (humans of unknown type who hunted the giant bison during the Ice Age some 8-10,000 years ago) were discovered nearby in White Horse Gulch by a cowboy in 1908. It is speculated that Folsom Man disappeared when severe drought brought extinction to the bison.

A few more miles to the west is the town of Raton, gateway to New Mexico on the main artery of the Santa Fe Trail. From the summit of Raton Pass, the Land of Enchantment unfurls like a storybook setting: the flatlands, the mesas, and ultimately, the spectacular mountain crests.

A largely untouched wilderness lies to the southwest of Raton, an area of wild and woolly flavor encompassing a variety of scenes. The snow-capped peaks are in view, framing the thick forests, placid meadowland, and scarred canyons. The Philmont Scout Ranch, an operating cattle ranch founded in the thirties by oilman Waite Phillips, is host to Explorer Scouts across the nation who arrive each year to learn the arts of horsemanship, survival and trail skills, and experience first-hand the thrill of true wilderness. Philmont, 127,000 acres of grasslands, mesas, rocky cliffs and lush forest, is also the site of the home of revered mountain man Kit Carson, a key figure in New Mexico's tempestuous history.

Just east of Philmont is a spot preserved forever in the continuing lore and lure of the Old West. The town of Cimarron, setting for countless movies and novels, perches at the entrance to the mountains and classic canyon of the same name. "Cimarron" is a Spanish reference to the big-horn sheep which were once plentiful here. The Cimarron Range includes Baldy and Touch-Me-Not Mountains, the north and south summits, respectively, and both over 12,000 feet. There are no roads across the rugged high country and some of the major peaks have had no contact with modern man short of an infrequent climber.

Cimarron itself is actually a pair of towns. "New Town" is the development along US 64 north of the river. "Old Town," on State 21 a mile to the south, though uninhabited now, was a nefarious social center of saloons and gunplay in the mid-1800s. It was here that land baron Lucien Maxwell, Old Cimarron's most prestigious and certainly wealthiest resident, erected his opulent Western-style

Gran Quivira National Monument
(Following pages) Soapweed yucca on a snowy New Mexico desert

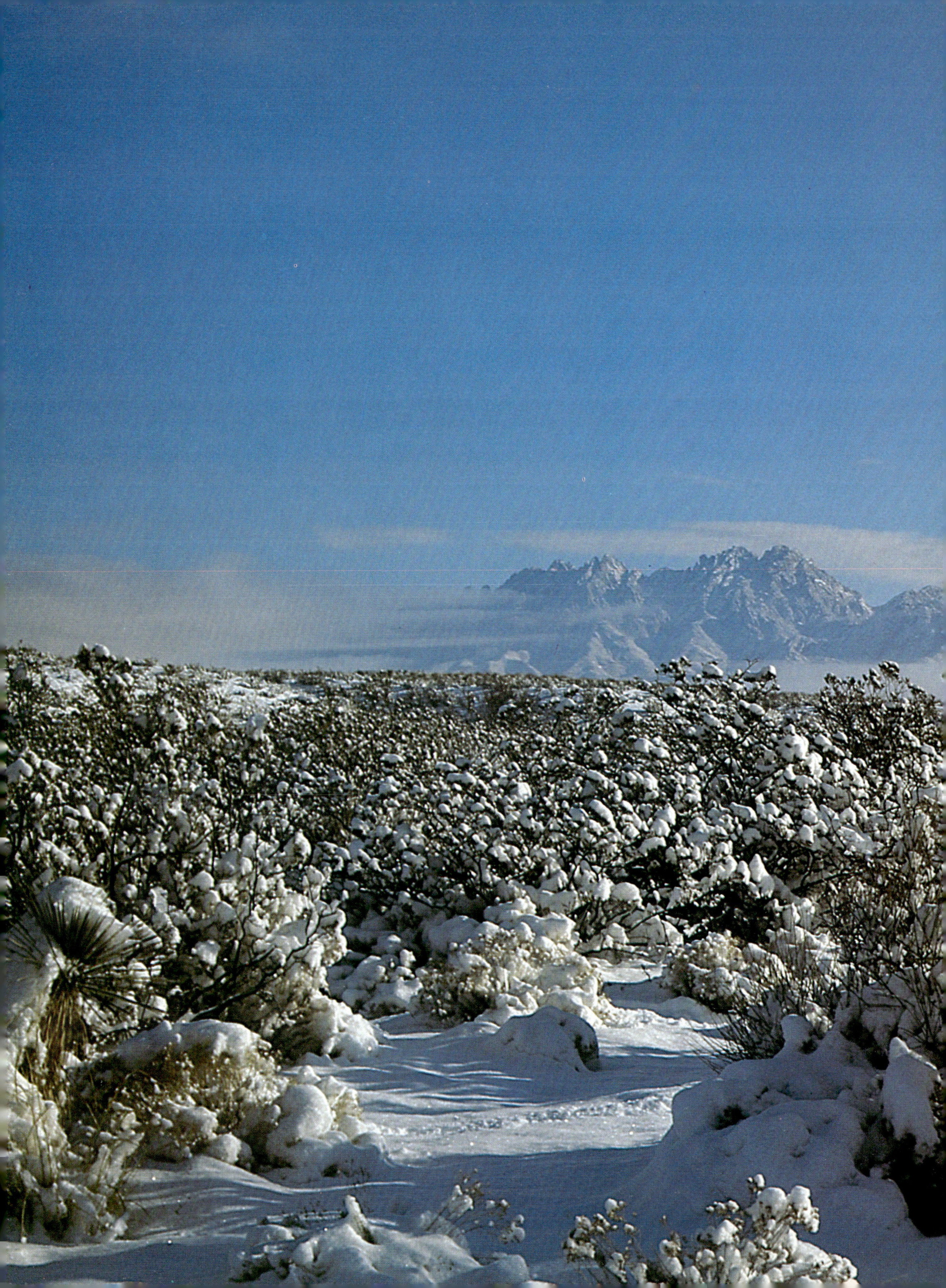

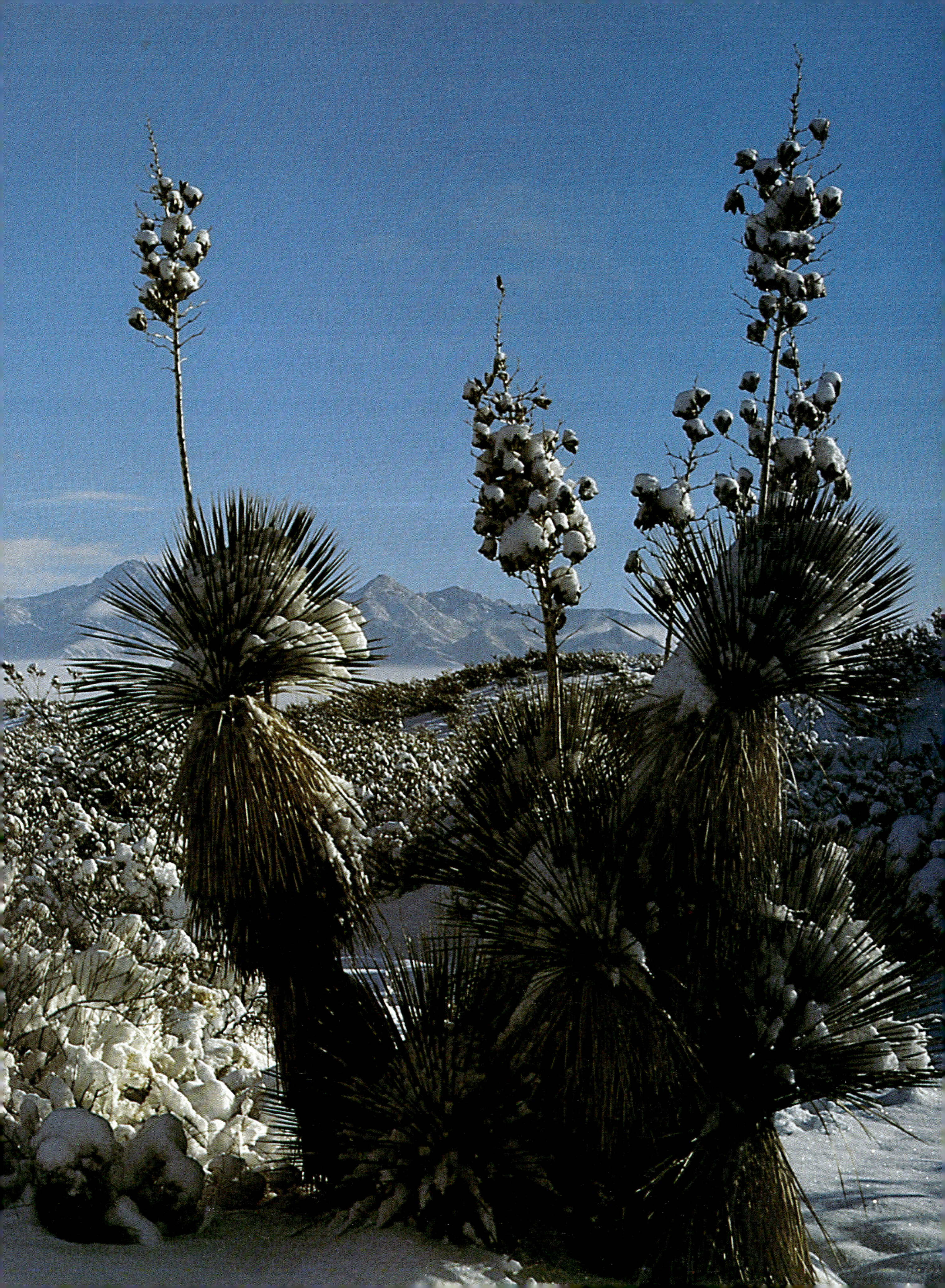

Starvation Peak near Las Vegas, New Mexico

Cholla cactus near the Rio Grande, south of Taos

palace. Today in New Town, Maxwell, now a statue of fitting proportions, sits with a shotgun across his lap, a reminder of days gone forever.

Cimarron may be the most celebrated ghost town in this part of the state, but it is by no means the only one. About 11 miles east on the Vermejo River, a dilapidated hotel at Colfax rests abandoned at the junction of US 64 and State 234. The hotel marks the way to Dawson, once a prosperous coal town in this valley of juniper and pinyon bounded by gently dappled hills on either side. Elizabethtown, on the wide hilltop near Eagle Nest, was the first incorporated town in the New Mexico Territory. Now a ghosted ruin, "E-Town" boomed with copper and gold in the 1860s. South of the Cimarron area, beyond the Turkey Mountains, is the site of Loma Parda. Still another ghost town, this one had the dubious distinction of being hailed as the Old West's Capitol of Vice, and not far away, Fort Union, once a key haven for travelers on the Santa Fe Trail.

East and south of the old adobe houses of Las Vegas (the largest town in these parts), the caprock plateau drops off abruptly, yielding to the plains and the mighty Canadian River with its marvelous lakes, notably the Conchas and Ute Reservoirs.

Carlsbad Caverns

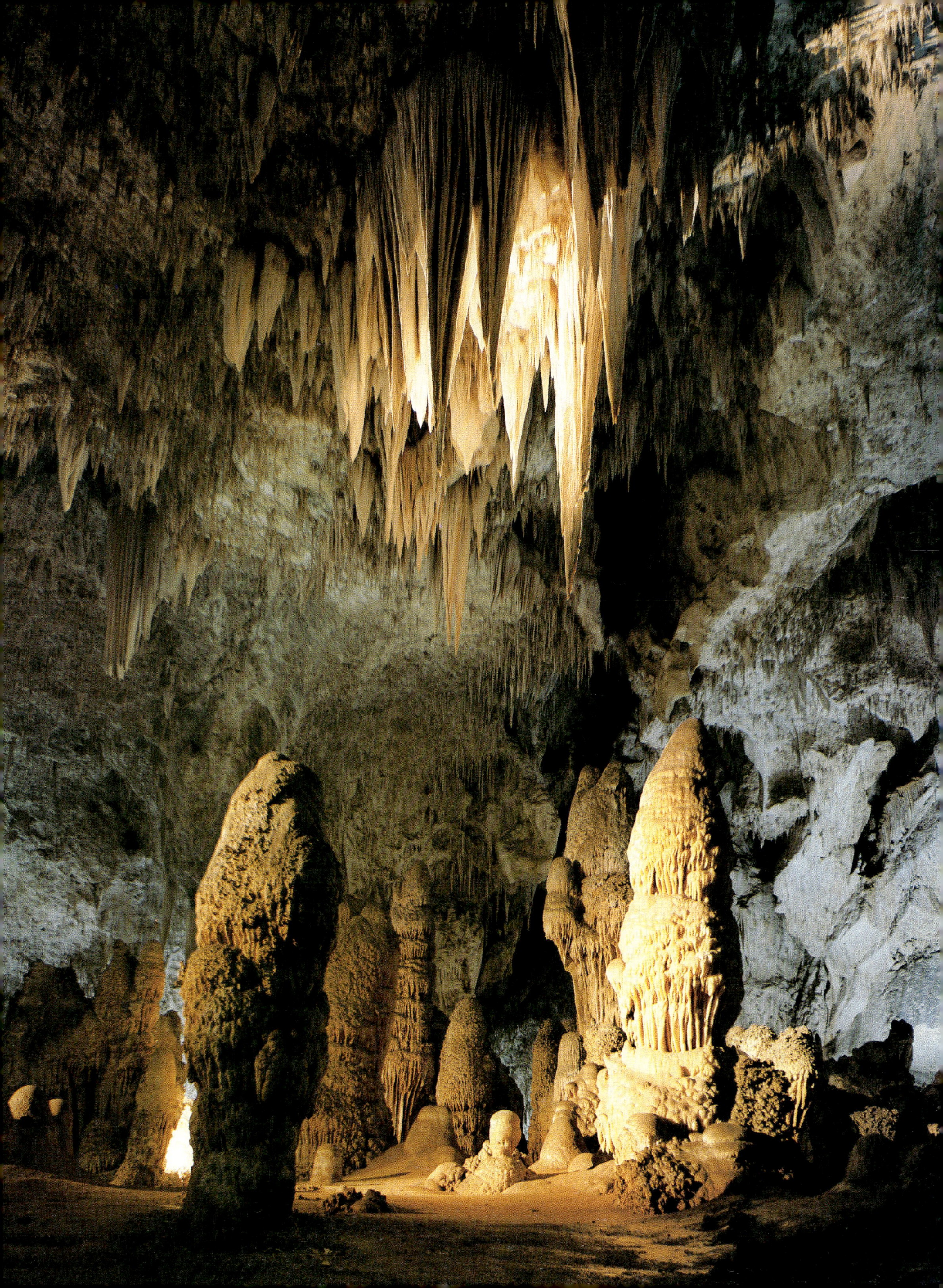

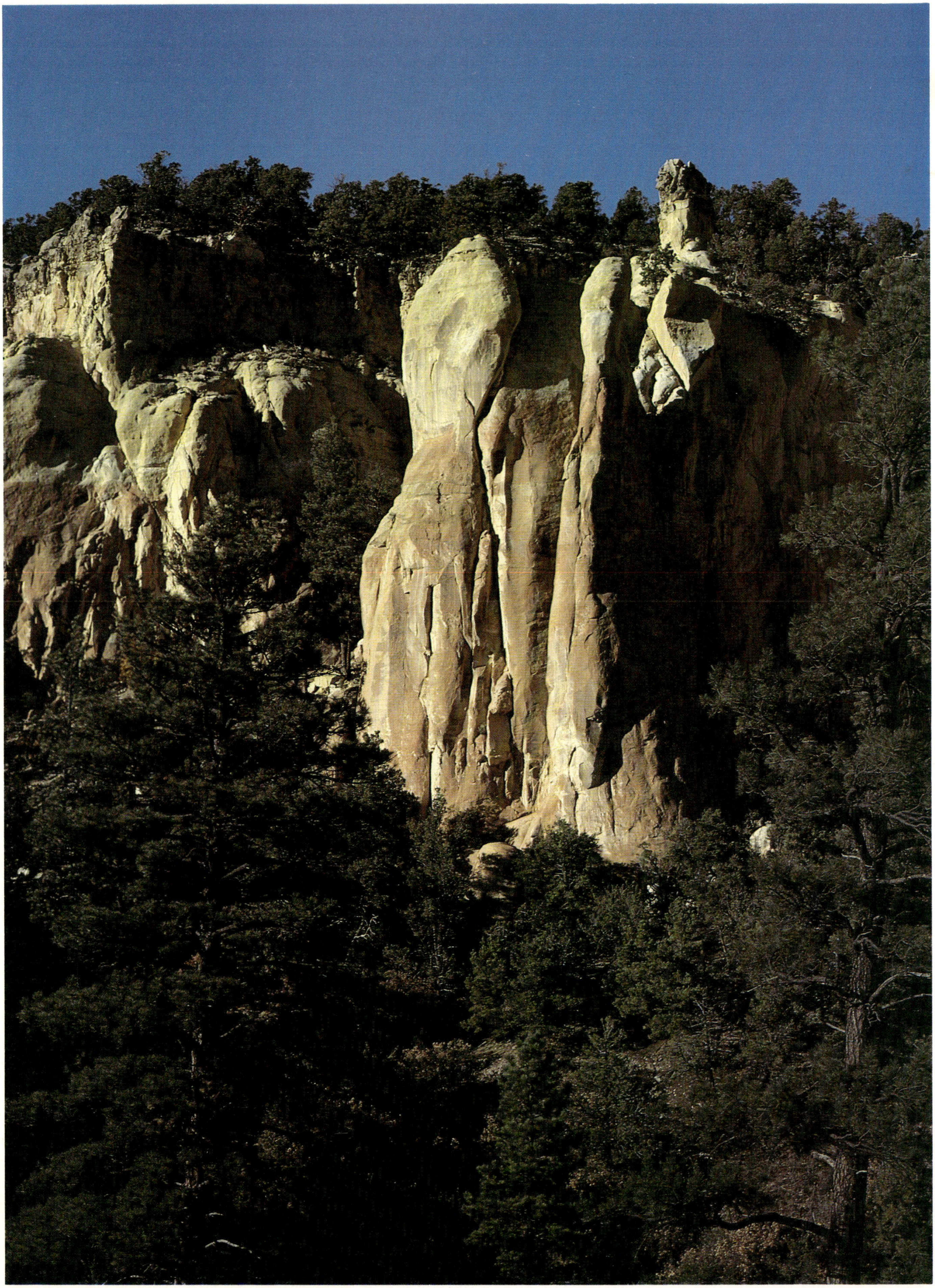

Organ Mountains silhouette the sunrise
(Following pages) The city lights of Los Cruces at sunset

Rock Formations near Gallina

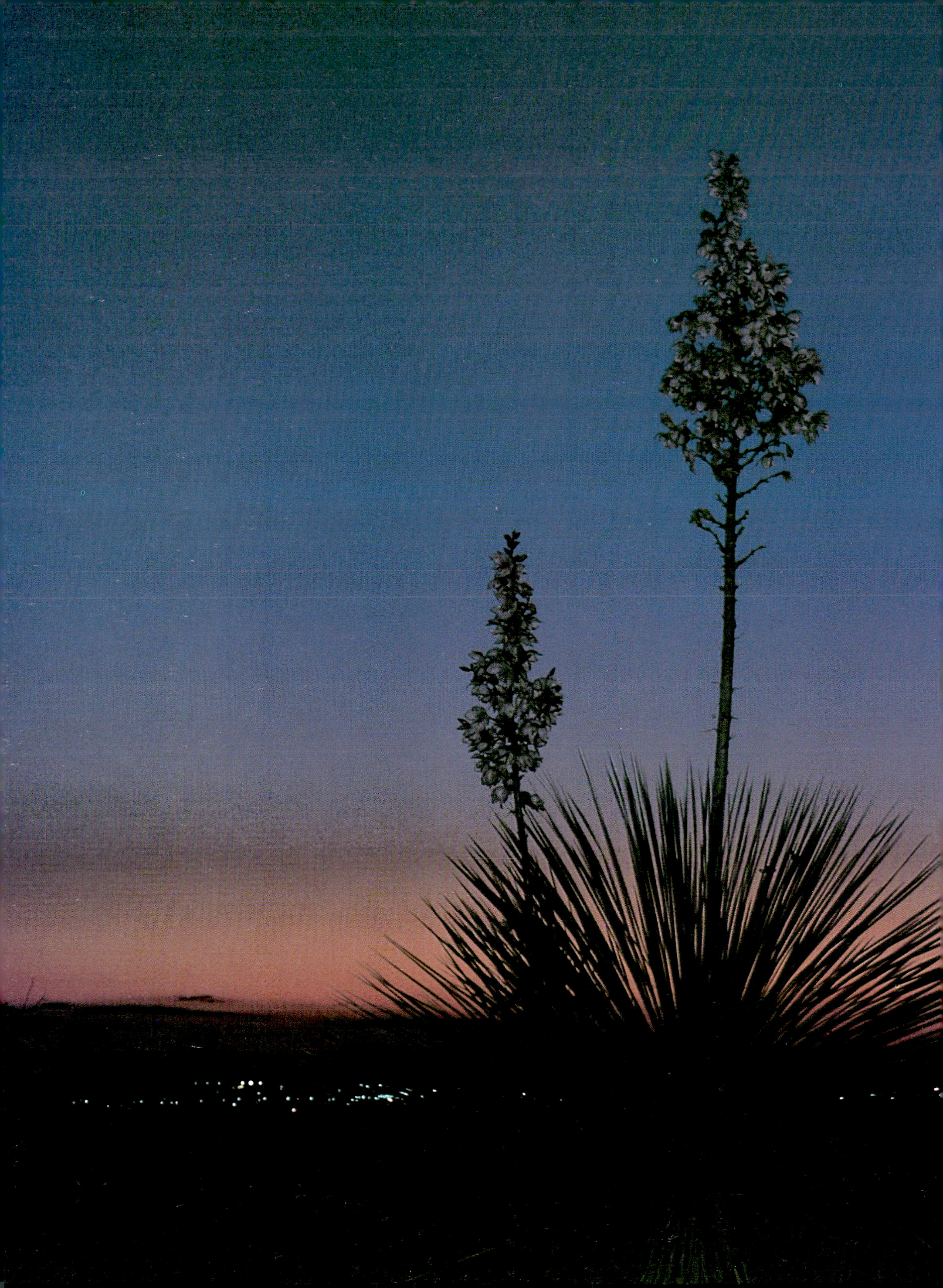

Apache plume

A mountain stream near Los Alamos

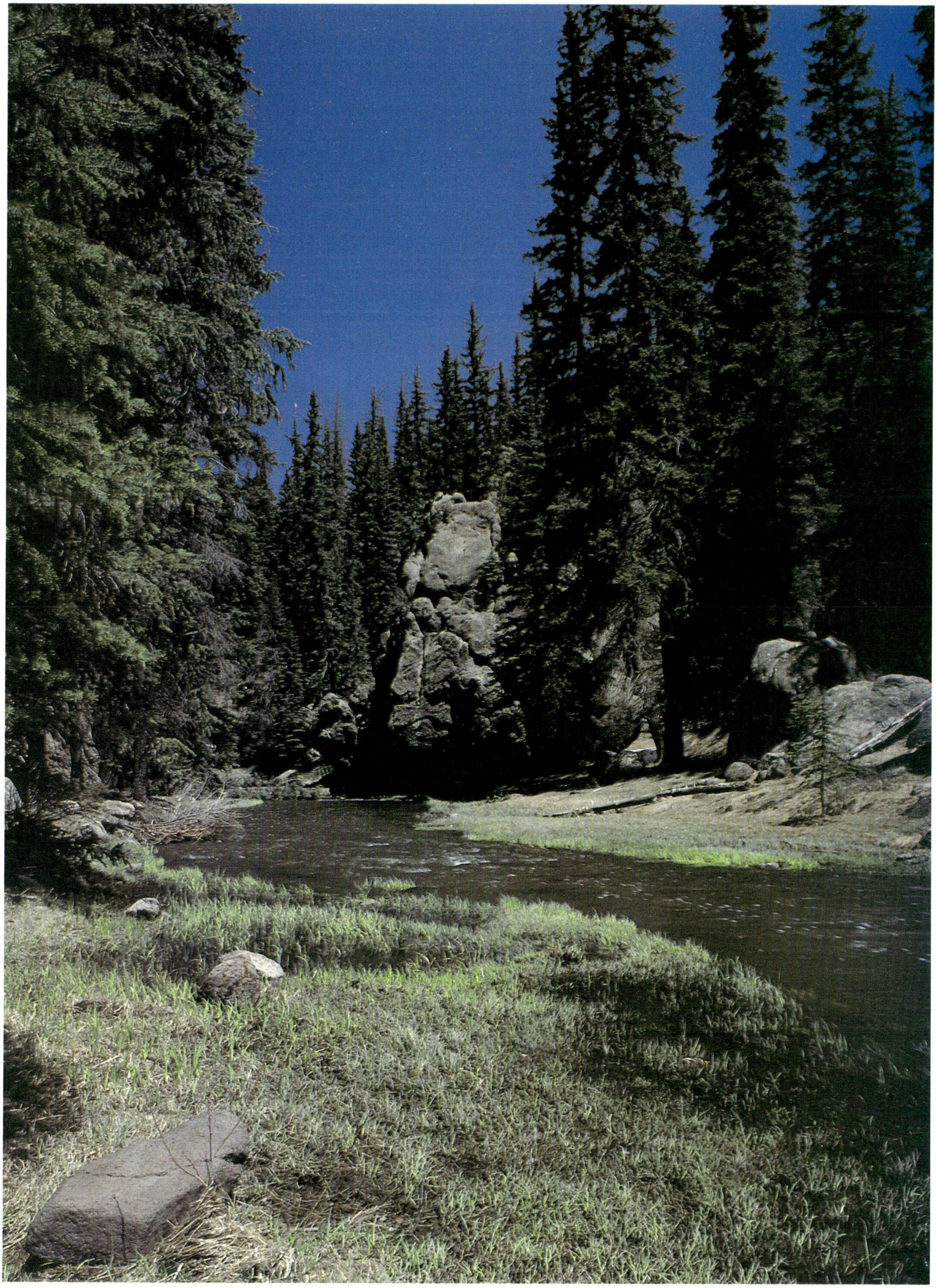

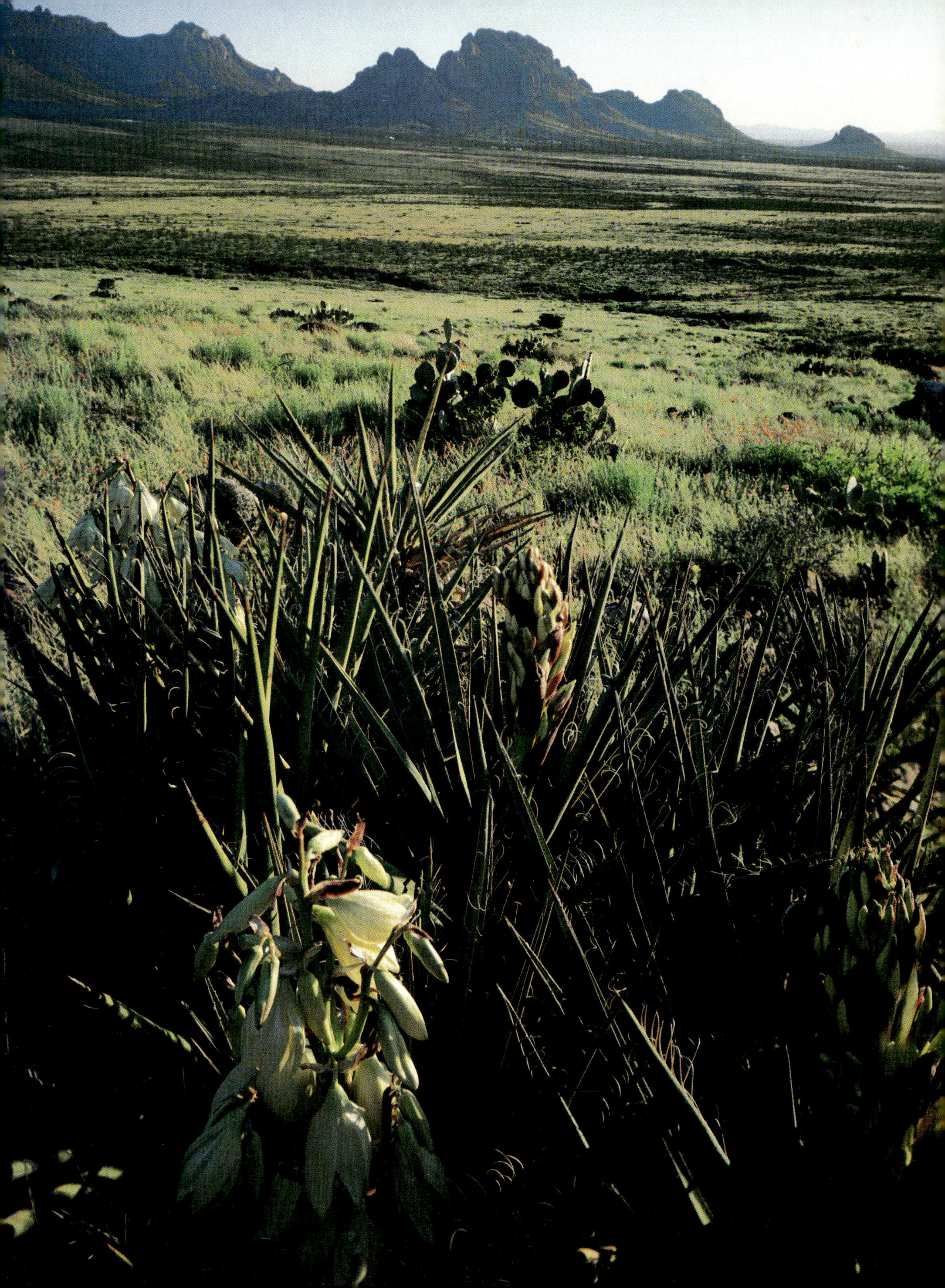

Northwest— Navajo Land to the Mesas of Acoma

This region of New Mexico, from the Colorado line to south Valencia County, is steeped in contradiction. It is one of the driest, most ruggedly desolate chunks of country anywhere. Yet it is as grand and spectacular a place as you're likely to find. Due to the aridity, it has been singularly unproductive land, and those who live here have had to work unceasingly to subsist. Sparsely inhabited, it is the Indian center of the United States and, as such, showcase for the most glorious spectacles and celebrations of the native American people. If there is an especially enchanted quadrant of New Mexico, then surely this is it.

Enter New Mexico from the extreme northwest at the Four Corners area (the only point in the U.S. common to four states) and you are in the stark and haunting country of the Navajo Nation. The 16-million acre Navajo Reservation is the largest anywhere and one third of all Navajos are New Mexicans. Farming is all but impossible on most of the reservation land, and while irrigation projects have been instigated, main-reservation Navajos are primarily sheep and goat herders, cattle and horse ranchers and harvesters of timber. This is a tough land, but a handsome one, much revered for its beauty. And beauty becomes fused with religion for these proud people. The "Beautyway Chant" celebrates the soul: "I will be happy forever, nothing will hinder me. I walk with beauty..." But the Navajo has not been reluctant to modernize his world or assert himself in the tricky spheres of economics and politics. The past few decades have seen great changes among the Navajo. Reservation radios can dial a Navajo D.J. in Gallup, broadcasting Country and Western music in the native tongue.

The reservation runs south in a wide strip from the San Juan River to the forbidding wilds of Coyote Canyon. One hundred long miles of Highway 666 (north-

The Yucca, found near the Florida Mountains in Rockhound State Park

Santa Fe Baldy

Hedgehog Cactus

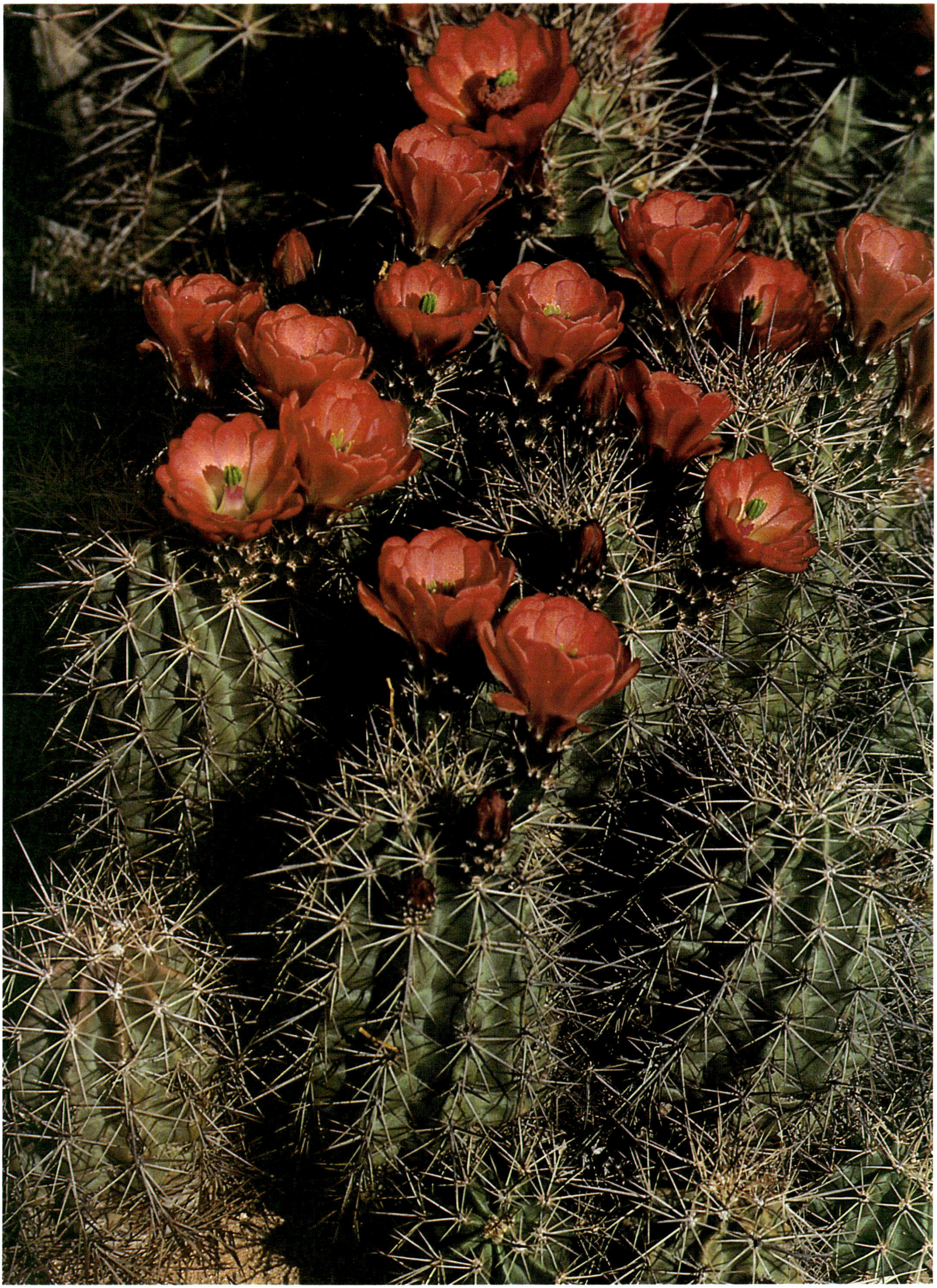

Sangre de Cristo Mountains

Yucca plant in the white sands

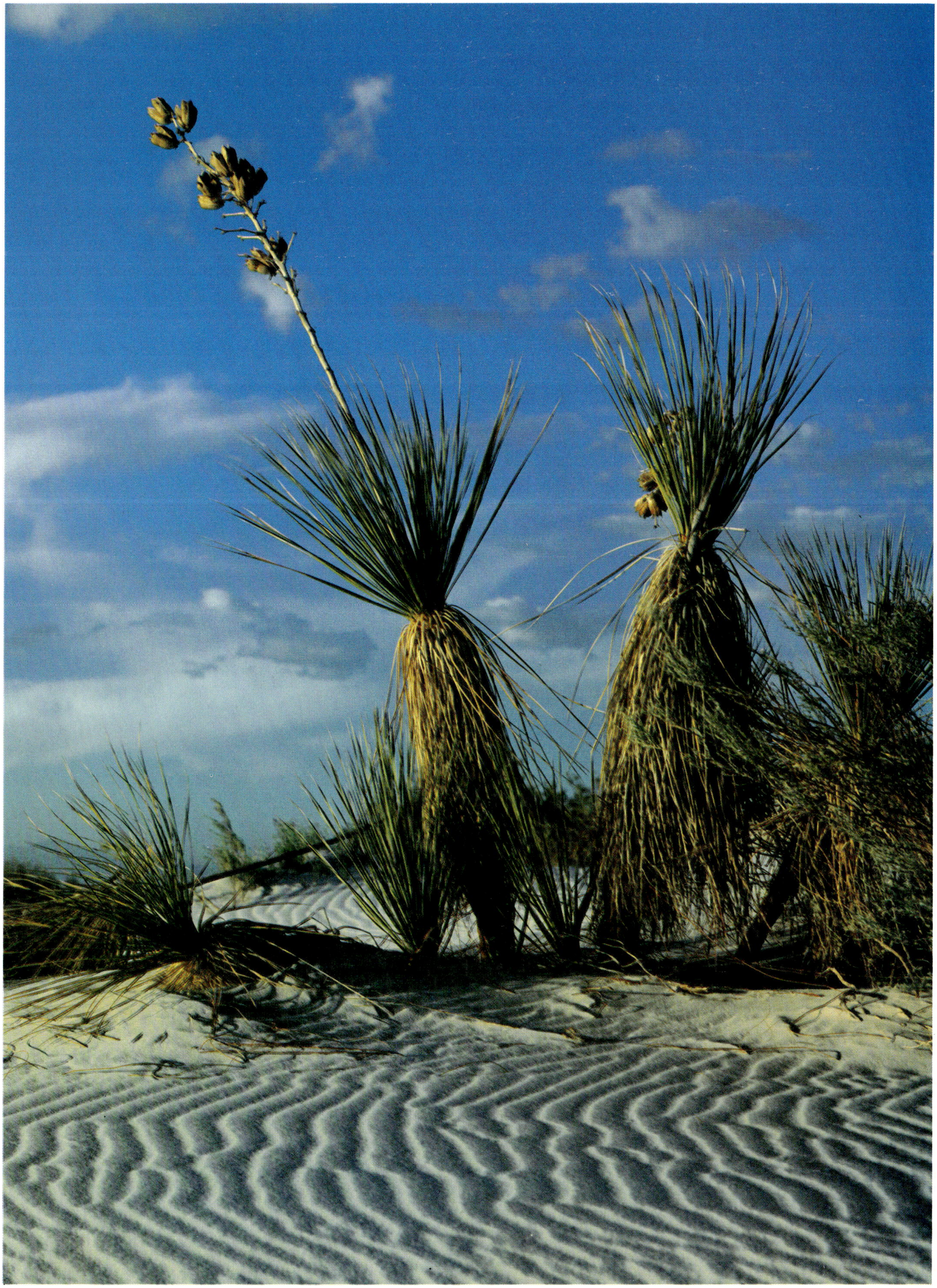

Wildflowers near Nogal Peak

Stone-walled ruins at El Morro National Monument

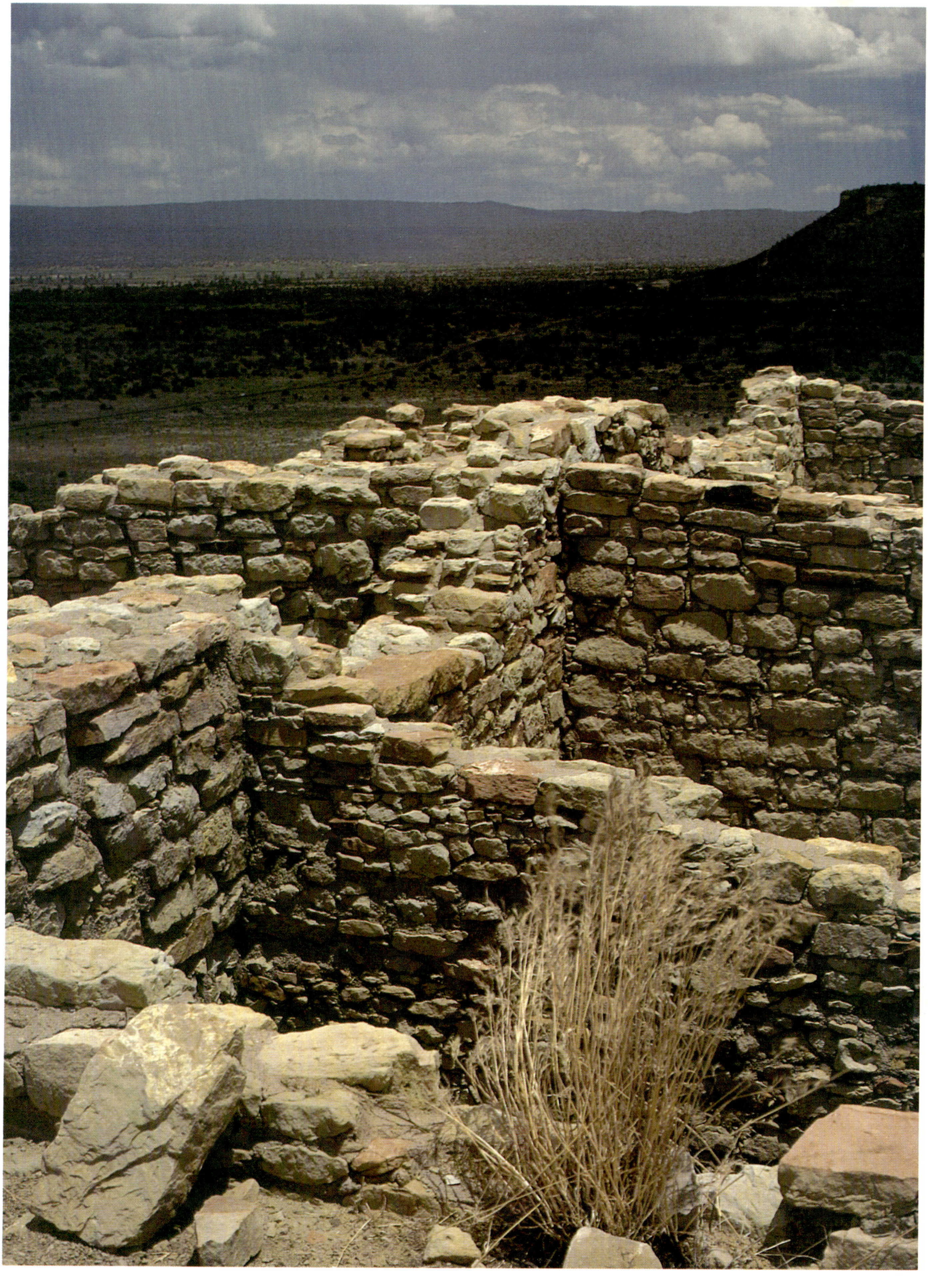

south) bisect the tribal holdings. The northern portions are rich with minerals: oil and natural gas wells are common and a significant amount of coal is mined here.

Not far from the junction of the highway and the river, the majestic monolith of Shiprock rears above the rough-grass flats. It is one of the state's best known and most photographed wonders. A volcanic masterpiece of grayish-brown spires, notches, sheer cliffs and sudden gullies, Shiprock towers 1,700 feet above the desert floor. In 1939, four members of the Sierra Club were the first climbers to reach the punishing summit. Though Shiprock's familiar profile conjures images of a great ocean vessel alive with a wind-filled cache of sails, the Navajos refer to it as *Tae-bidahi* (Rock with Wings) and hold it sacred. According to legend, Shiprock was once a huge, holy bird.

South along the highway, the red rock and buckled plains race to the horizon in all directions. Winding canyons, dry creek beds and dusty mountains weave through the reservation. The Chuska Range of quartz sandstone enters diagonally from Arizona where State Road 134 slices through at Washington Pass. This is a rarely seen pocket of New Mexico, a bleak spectacle of strange and bewitching rock formations. The Valley of the Obelisks in the southern Chuskas sprouts slim columns of sandstone rushing skyward for hundreds of feet. One such spire is Venus Needle, a rocket of stone pointing resolutely toward the stars.

Just south of the Navajo Reservation is the town of Gallup, "Indian Capitol of the World." Surrounded by golden-bronze cliffs and treacherous badlands, Gallup hosts the well-attended Intertribal Indian Ceremonial each August. Further south is the reservation of the Zuni Indians (a Pueblo group known for the exacting handicraft work in turquoise and silver), one of the most fascinating spots on earth in late fall when the spectacular religious ceremony, The Shalako, is enacted. This annual return of the "Council of the Gods" sets off a riotous 24 hours of continuous dancing and feasting.

East of Zuni is El Morro National Monument. At first sight, El Morro (The Headland), appears to be a huge outcrop of solid limestone casting shadows on the gently rolling plains below. In fact, it is a giant-box or bowl, with sides shooting 200 feet up and forming a perfect canyon within. A 700-year-old pueblo sits on the mesa rim and at the base is a rare fresh-water pool to explain why western-bound travellers have for centuries visited this spot. And ever since the Pueblos scratched their petroglyphs in the walls of Inscription Rock, untold numbers of passersby have signed the limestone ledger. The first European to attach his signature was Don Juan de Onate, the original Spanish colonizer, who took this route in 1605 in his quest for the "Sea of the South."

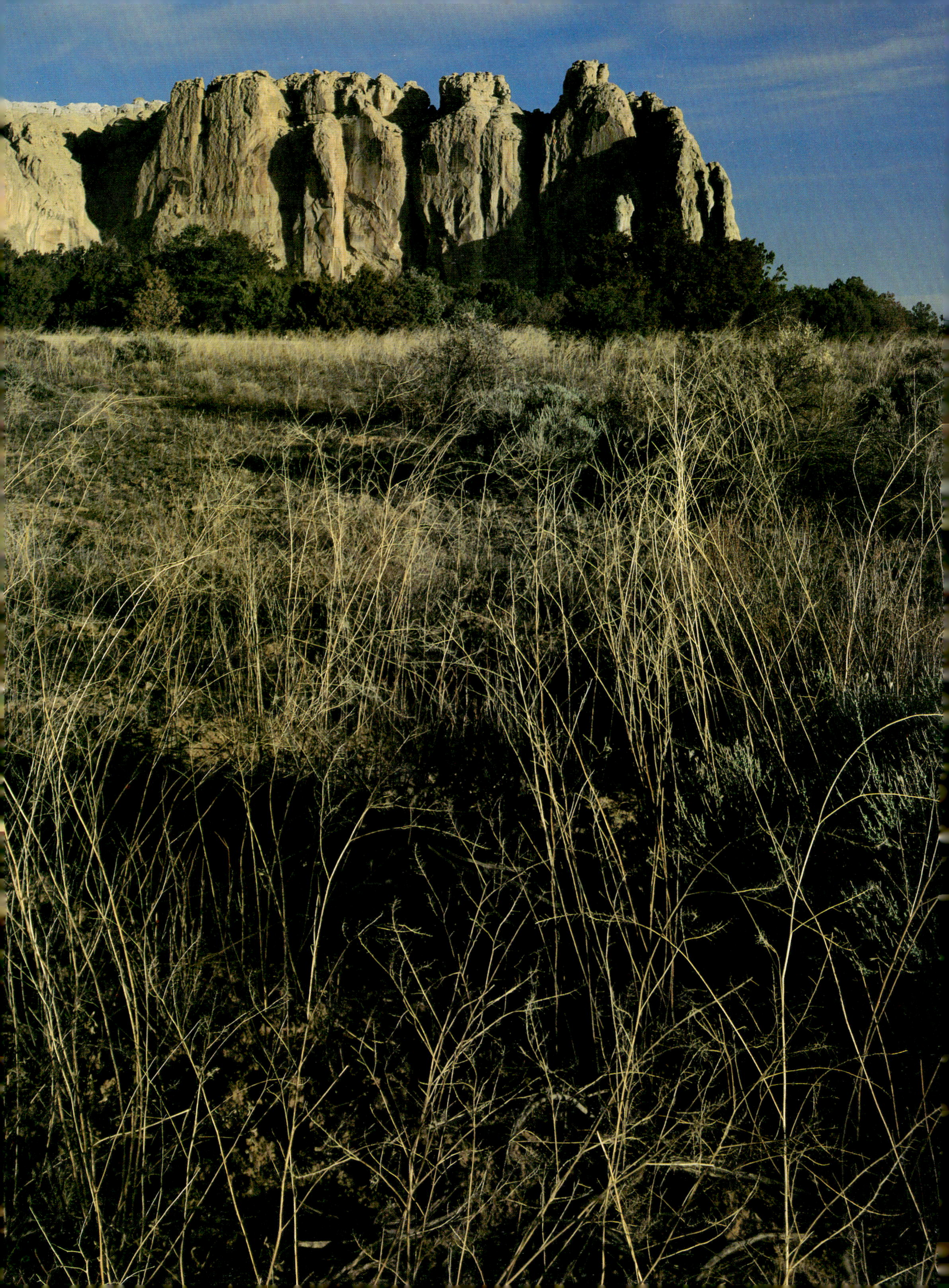

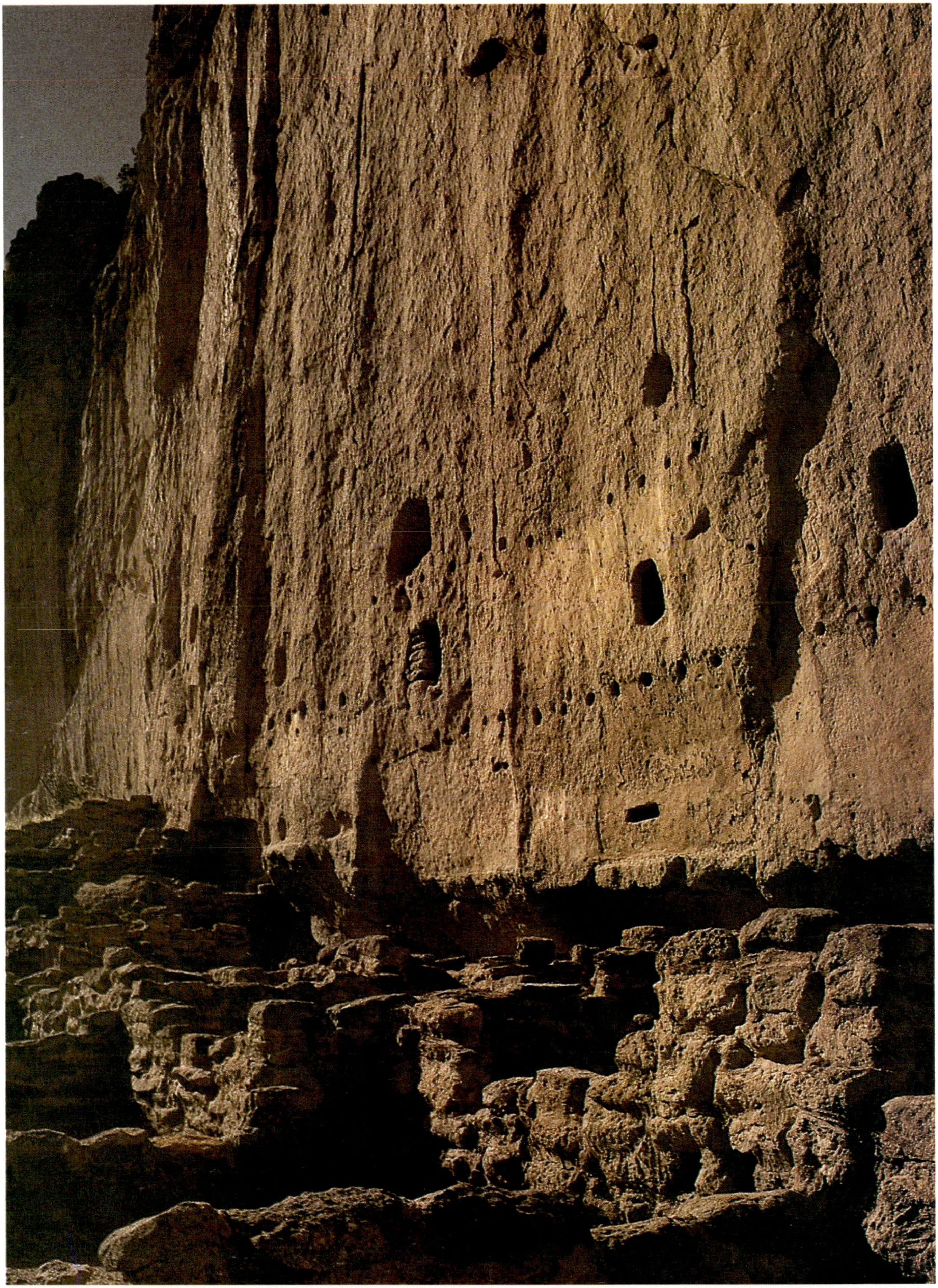

To the east on I-40 (formerly the celebrated Route 66) is Grants, once merely a station on the Santa Fe Railway, now the capitol of the uranium mining industry. The surrounding land is bordered on either side by the remote reaches of the Cibola National Forest.

On the western side of Grants is the home of the legendary Pueblo group, the Acomas. Atop the massive 400-foot sandstone mesa perches the "Sky City" of Acoma. Indians began living here as early as 900 A.D. The eroded cliffs plummet on all sides to the green valley below, creating a fine natural fort and an unparalleled view of the surrounding mesa country. The Acomas were farmers, stockmen and crafters of delicately exquisite pottery. Their city in the sky is a worthy example of architecture wedded to the environment: the pueblo seemingly carved from the plateau top, with ceremonial kivas among the dwelling units.

The landscape here holds a great number of astonishing rock masses and among them, a few miles from Acoma Pueblo, is enchanted Mesa. It stands 430 feet above the reservation, an isolated stone of pale, salmon-color appearing particularly treacherous and foreboding. The Acomas claim to have inhabited the mesa top long ago and tell of a tragic stranding of some tribe members when the only trail down was erased by a savage storm. Today they shun the spot and cite disembodied wailing voices heard around the sheer walls as reason for staying away.

Two rivers snake through these desertlands: the Rio San Jose runs west along the route of I-40 and, veering away, the Rio Puerco. Following the latter, a number of miles to the north is the volcanic neck of Cabezon and to the east the holdings (¾ of a million acres) of the Jicarilla Apaches in the mountainlands.

In the waterless central portions of northwest New Mexico, a largely uninhabited wilderness of crusty canyons, severely eroded tableland and barren flats, are the prehistoric ruins of enigmatic Chaco Canyon. Who were the builders of this obviously advanced cluster of buildings and tunnels? How did they survive? When did they abandon the area and where did they go? The mystery persists. There are similar constructions and scenic puzzles at Salmon ruins near Bloomfield, and beyond, at the Aztec Ruins National Monument.

(Following pages) White Sands National Monument

Long house ruins, Bandelier National Monument

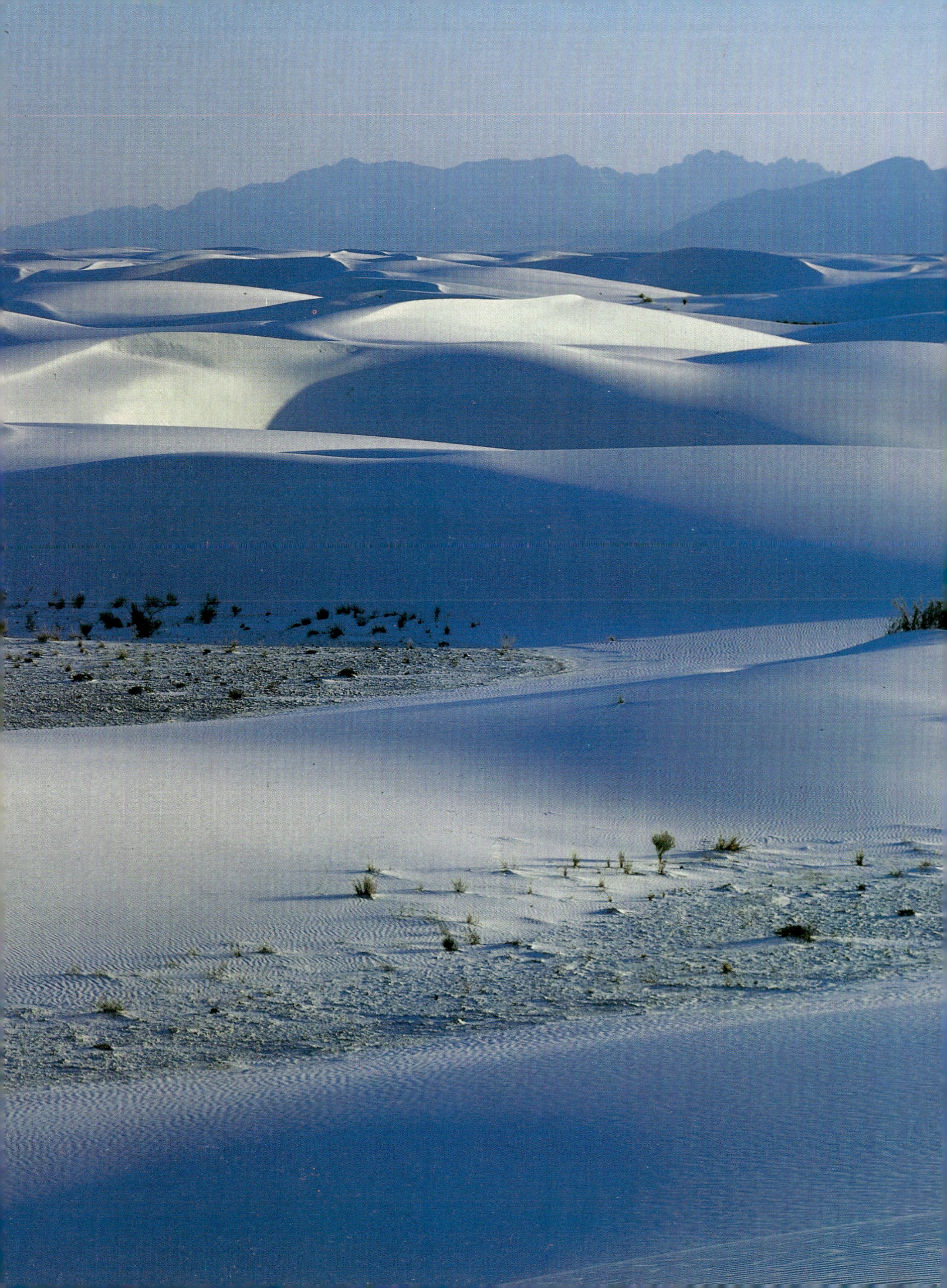

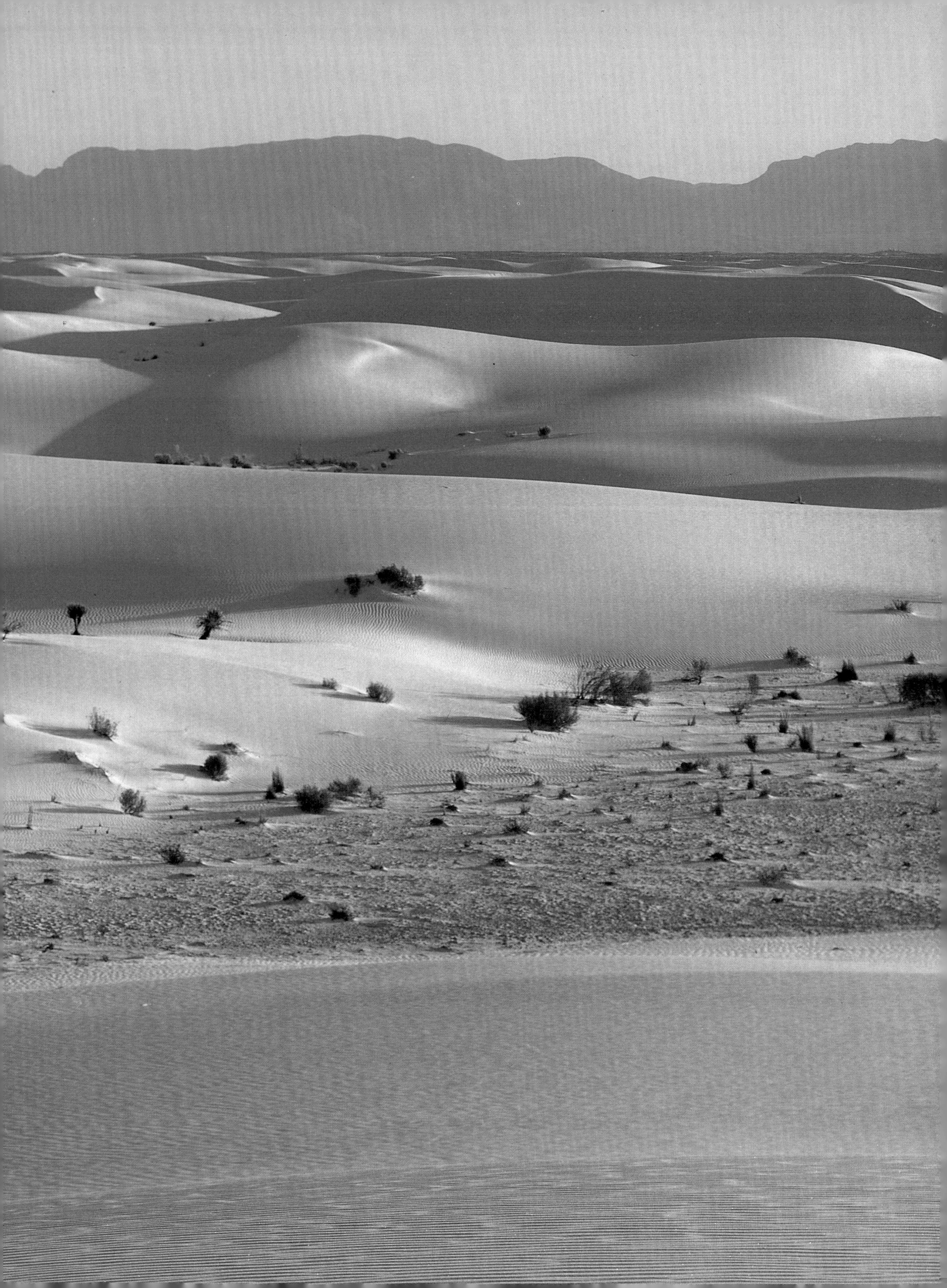

Organ Mountains near Los Cruces

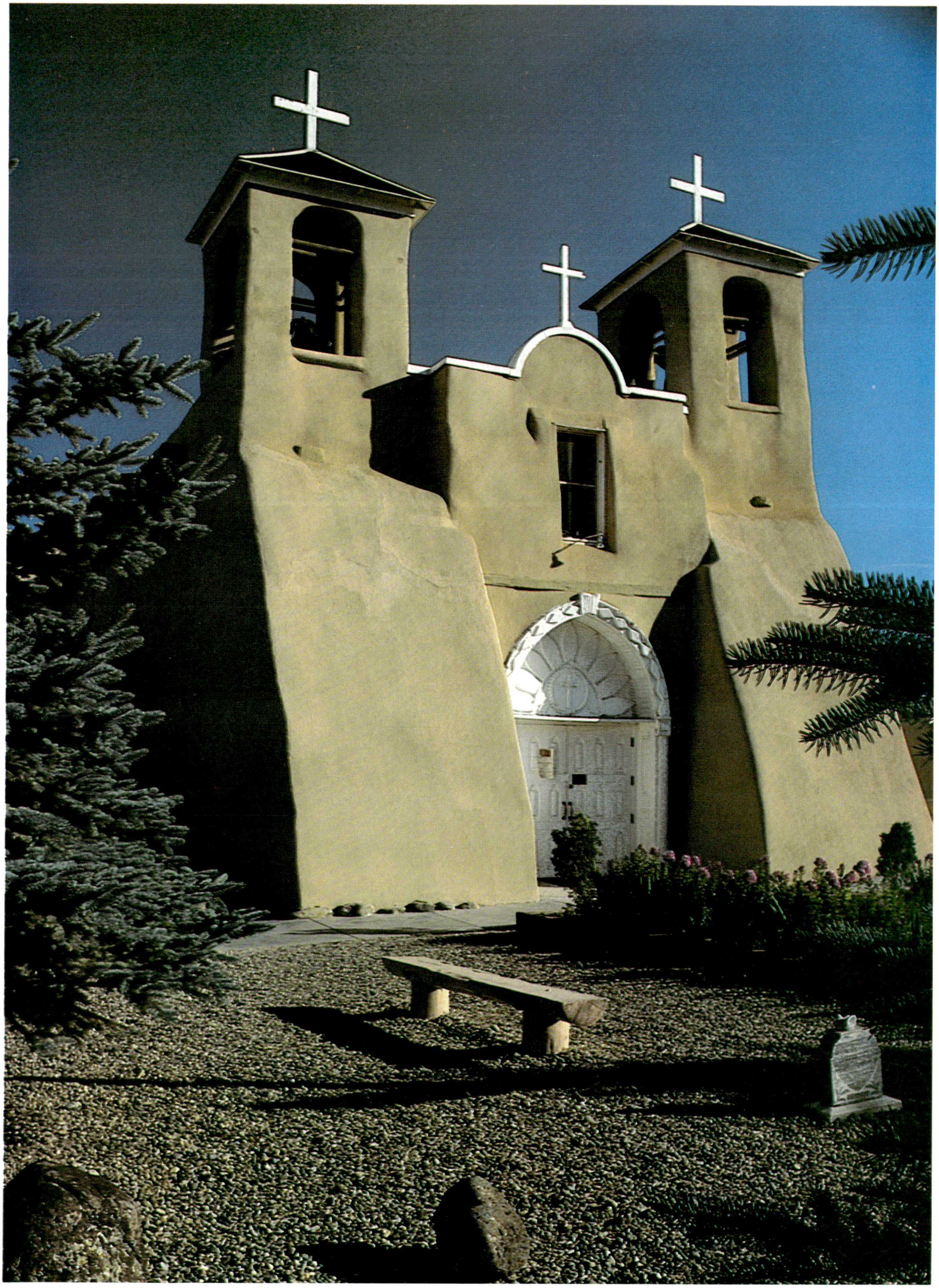

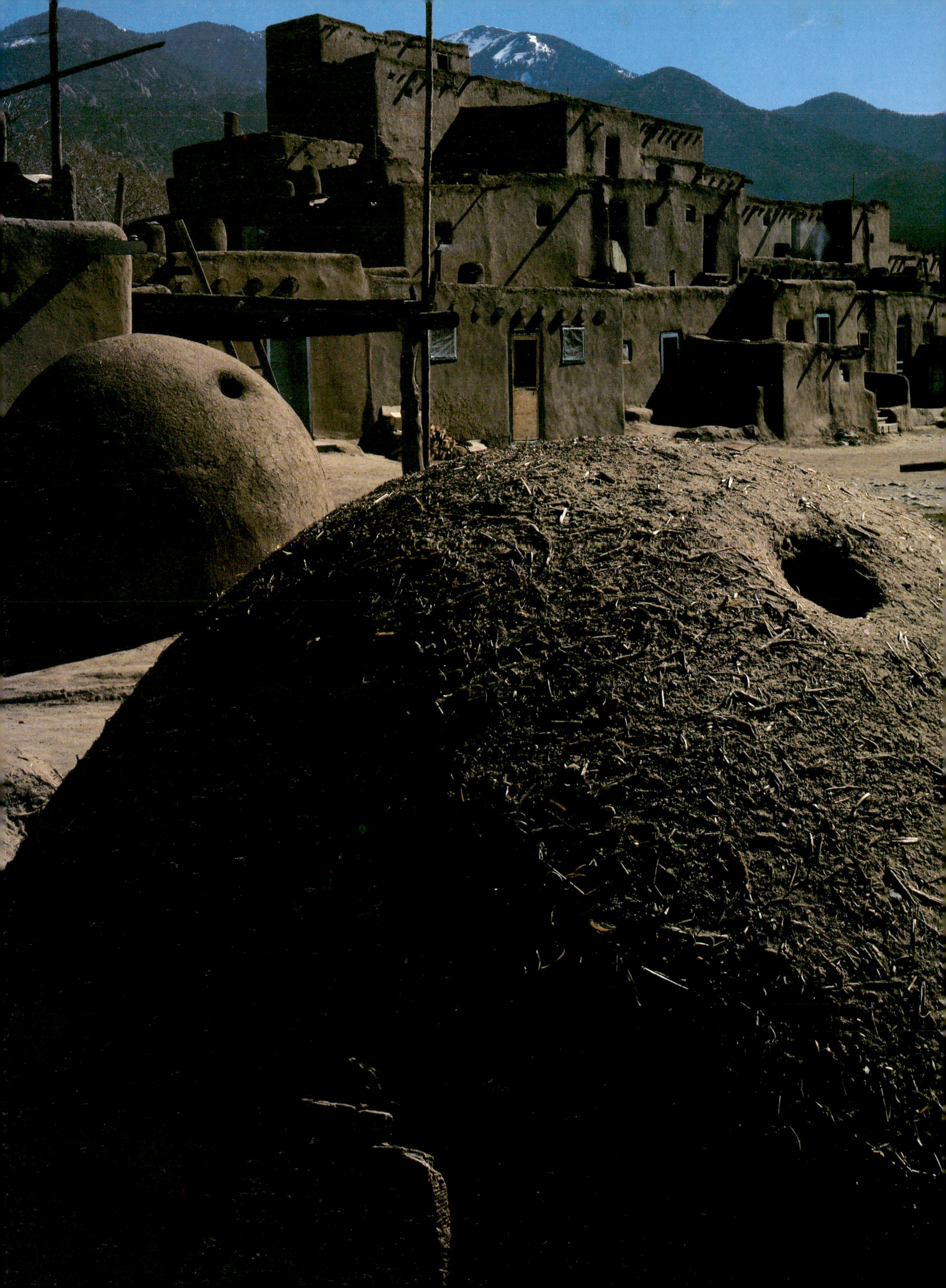

Southwest—
Gila Wilderness to
the Rio Grande

Water has long been a major concern in New Mexico. There's just not enough of it to go around. Rainfall around the state averages a scant 9 to 16 inches per year. Indians danced for it, Spaniards prayed for it, but appeals to the heavens were not enough. The answer, instead, was irrigation, and today the fertile valley of the Rio Grande is proof that even the dustiest of deserts can be made to bloom with abundance. The river crashes down from the mountains and is siphoned off to farms and orchards on its way south, reduced to little more than a trickle in mid-summer.

The pleasant town of Soccorro in the northern section of this fertile ribbon, once a rough and tumble Western outpost, is agriculture-minded today. And although fruits and vegetables are the leading by-products of the Rio Grande, recreation is a close second. Elephant Butte Reservoir, north of Truth or Consequences, is the most impressive of the great river's lakes: cool, blue waters alive with gamefish encircle the gray butte while the bare ridges of the Fra Cristobal Range camp on the western skyline. And it's worth mentioning the Bosque del Apache Wildlife Refuge located between Soccorro and the lake. The San Marcial marshes, once a winter haven for Apache war parties, have since been preserved as an ornithologist's dreamland. If you arrive in winter, you are in the company of half a million birds: flocks of Canadian snow geese, sandhill cranes, the rare whooping cranes and Mexican black duck, and hundreds of other varieties.

The key city on the bottom half of the Rio Grande lies to the south where I-25 and I-10 cross—Las Cruces. Here the charm of Old Mexico is preserved with undeniable style and grace. The original settlement in the area is known as La Mesilla and many a weary traveller has found refuge in the shady plaza. The river is especially productive here. Miles of lettuce and cotton fields span the area, and south of town grow the largest pecan orchards in the world.

Taos Pueblo

Organ Mountains

Chama Valley

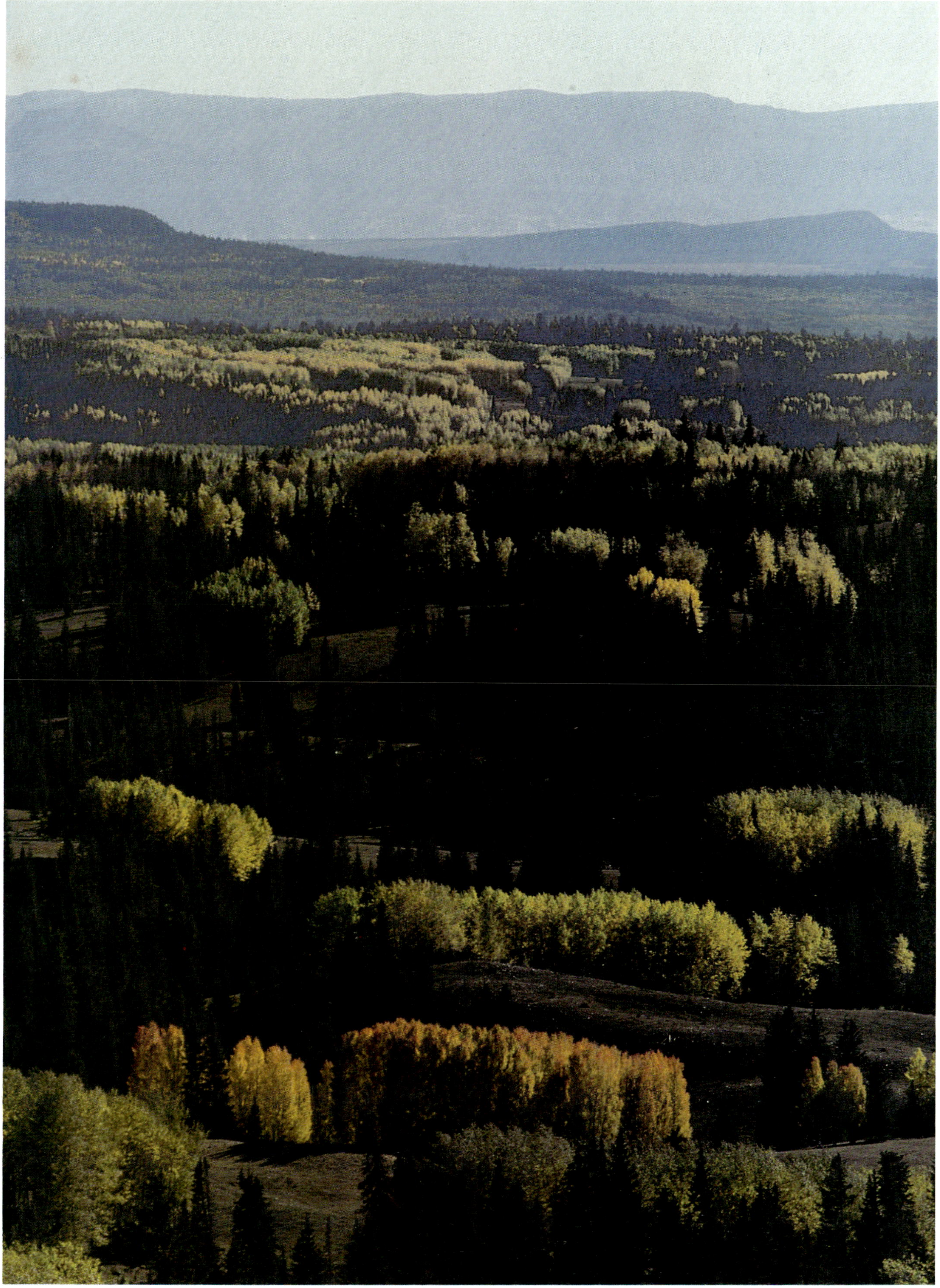

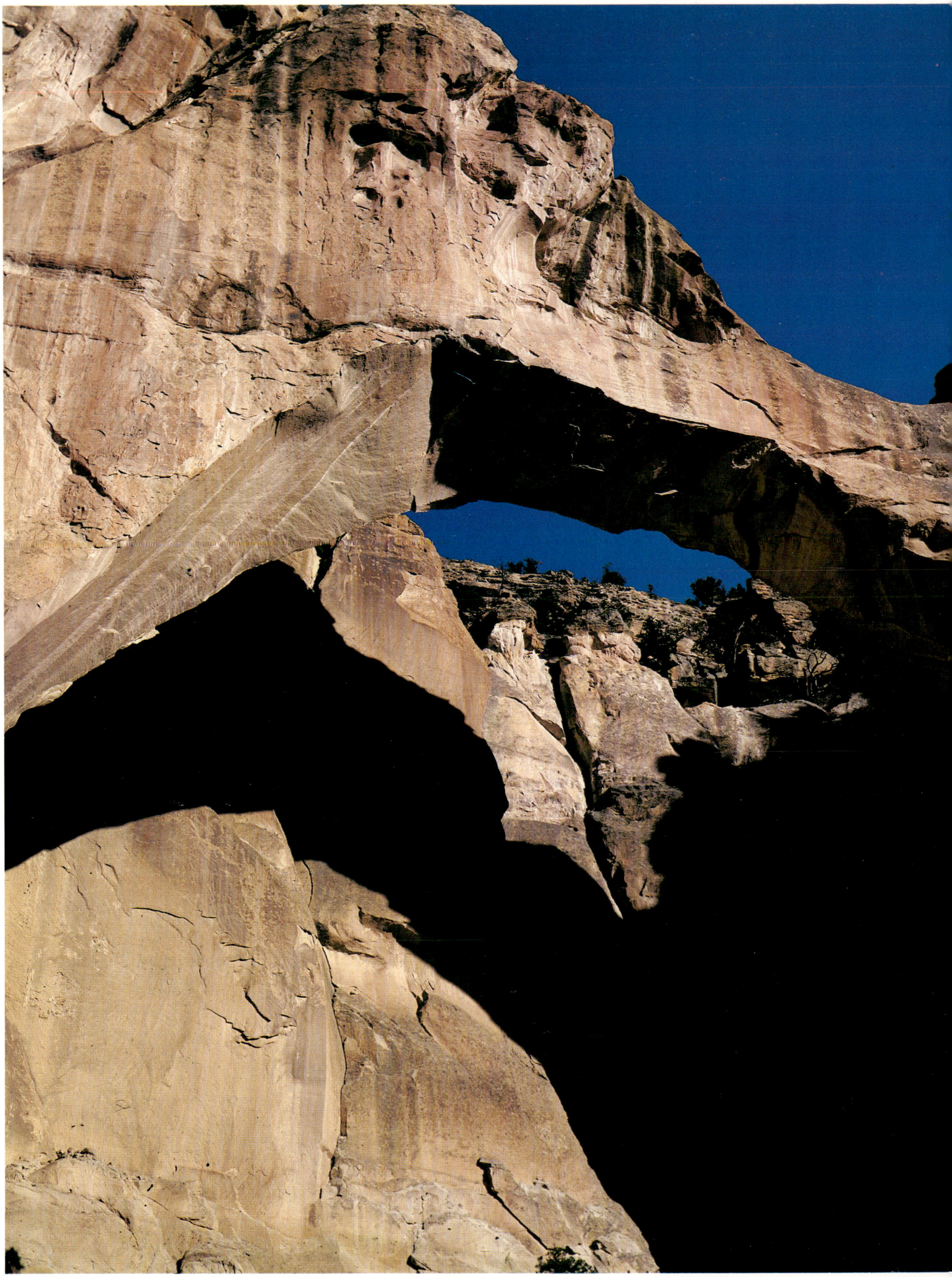

The natural stone arch located near Grant

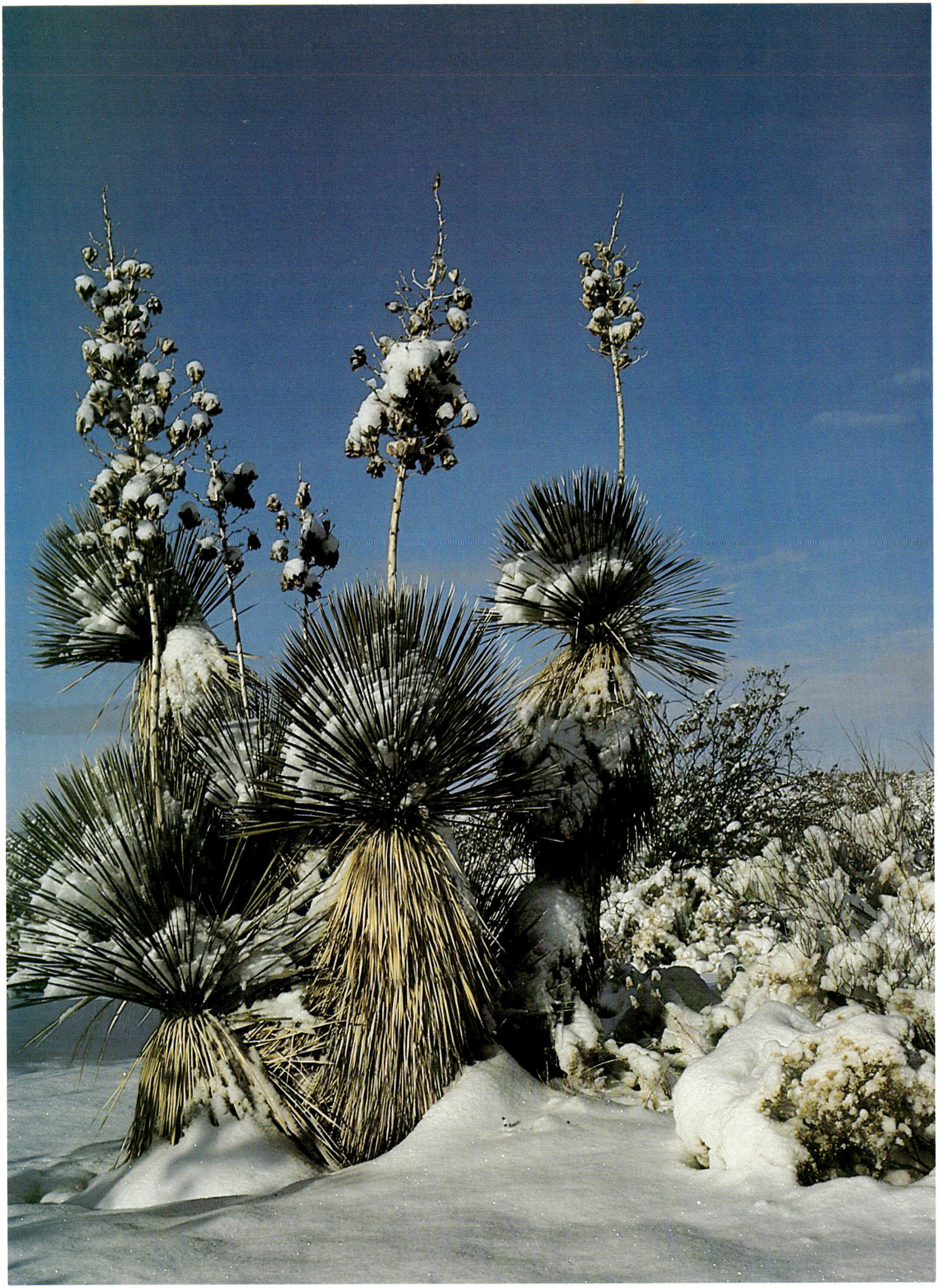

Soapweed yucca

Colorful mesa near Gallina

On the city's eastern skyline pose the jagged peaks of the Organ Mountains, so named for their resemblance to a kingly set of organ pipes. The original name was La Sierra de la Soledad (Mountains of Solitude) and it does much to describe the Organs. However, its needle-like promontories have become a supreme attraction for rock climbers and geologists, despite the inconveniences of thick cactus growth, loose stone, a healthy population of rattlesnakes and the total absence of water.

West of Las Cruces, Interstate 10 runs to the Arizona border through the railroad towns of Deming, Lordsburg and the curious ghost town of Shakespeare, where the old Stratford Hotel remains, looking much as it did in the silver boom days of the 19th century. South is New Mexico's boot-heel and the Hatchet Mountains, where prehistoric man was once at work mining turquoise. This is a wilderness as wild as they come. A gravel road runs down to Antelope Wells on the Mexican border, but the peaks are practically inaccessible. A 90,000-acre game preserve covers some of the mountains where big-horn sheep, antelope and white-tail deer roam among the yucca, prickly pear, agave, and cholla cactus.

North of I-10 in the foothills of the Pinos Altos range is the town of Silver City. As the name implies, the surrounding slopes were once mined for silver. Copper is still removed from the mountains today and, along with some cattle ranching, Silver City remains healthy. The town's second distinction is its role as gateway to the Gila Wilderness Area and miles of breathtaking forests, all virtually untouched.

The Gila is an immense region, taking in several mountain ranges and two huge national forests. The Black Range dominates the eastern portions. These slopes are typical of the dry forest throughout the area: bunchgrass-covered terrain broken by contorted, rocky outcrops and stands of pine and cottonwood. The settlements are remnants of gold bonanza days. There was a lot of silver too, and one natural cave known as Bridal Chamber that yielded three million dollars worth of the purest silver, so simple to mine that the lucky prospectors merely loaded up and hauled it out. The best-known ghost towns are located on the east edge of the Wilderness Area: Winston and Chloride. But a word of caution—all of New Mexico's ghost towns are not necessarily dead. Certain solitary souls, who have chosen the peace of the wilds to the city's hassles, occasionally occupy areas in and around ghost towns. Souvenir seekers have been known to "discover" what is thought to be a forgotten relic and innocently carry away the local resident's tools or furniture.

Perhaps the most spectacular of the Gila's mountains are the Mogollons in the west. Several of the rugged, sharply-contoured peaks rise above 10,000 feet. This was dangerous Apache country at one time, demanding terrain where only the stout-hearted and resourceful survived. Whitewater Canyon provided a hide-out not only for the legendary Geronimo, but also for Butch Cassidy and his gang.

Tree-covered mesa near Los Alamos

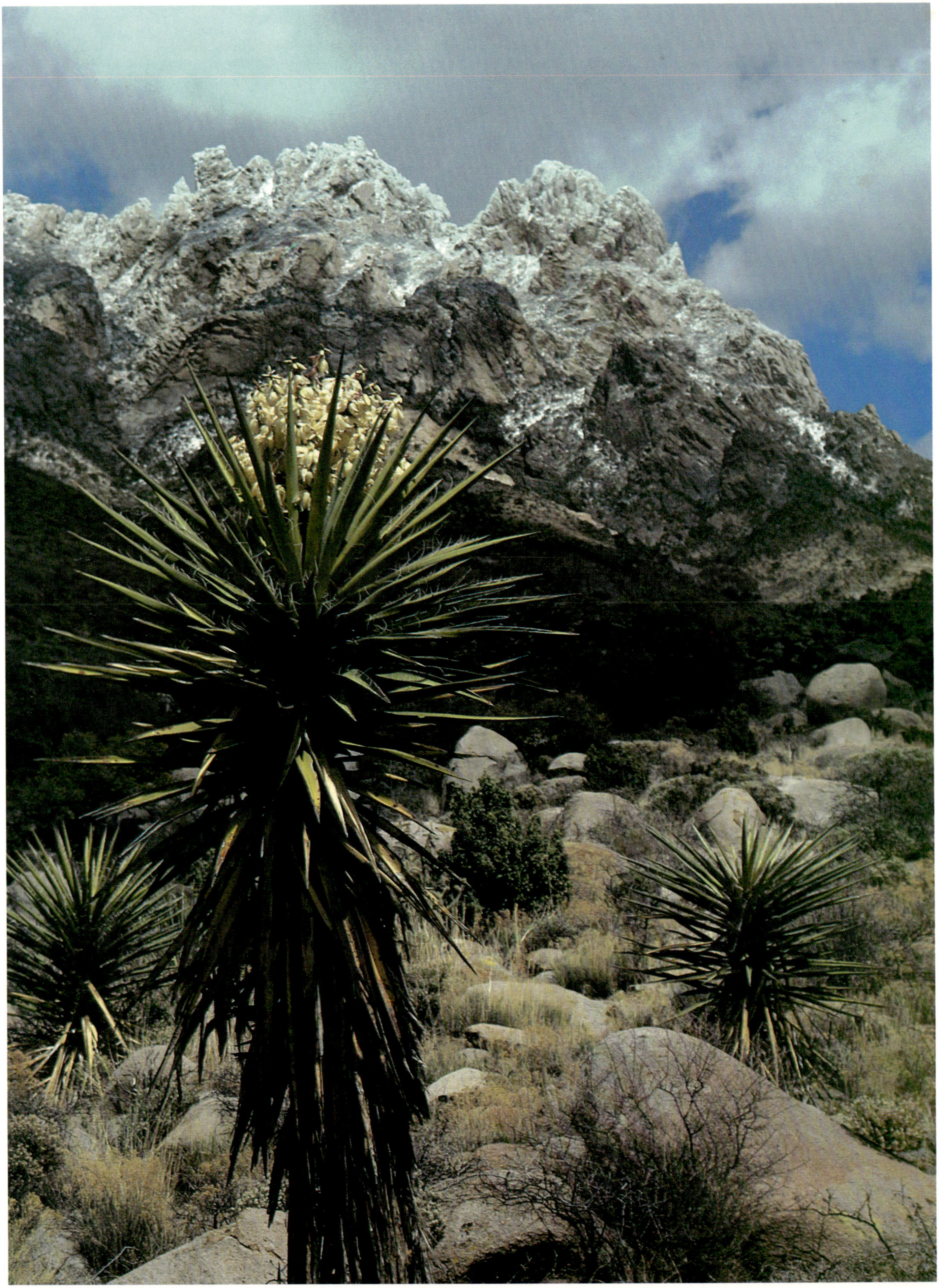

The town of Mogollon was the heart of the area during boom days and fell abandoned when the silver was gone. In its heyday, Mogollon was as colorful as any frontier town. There are tales of violence in such establishments as the Bloated Goat Saloon and the engaging legend of an old prospector who raised a grizzly bear from a cub, tamed it and took to riding it through town when he'd had enough whiskey.

The mountains in this part of New Mexico have everything the mountain lover could ask for. If you ever tire of just gazing on the miles of green forest, the deep gorges and lonely crags, there are hiking trails to explore, tumbling streams and rivers that feed occasionally into a serene lake. There are also momentos of past cultures: the Gila Cliff Dwellings and an unnervingly slender walkway skirting the cliffs above Whitewater Canyon, called The Catwalk.

In the northern portions of the Gila Wilderness is the small town of Reserve, an ironic name considering its reputation in the days of the Old West and Elfego Baca. Baca, at age 19, single-handedly shot it out with a hostile gang of 80 Texas cowboys who had been terrorizing the Spanish-speaking residents. In a building the size of an outhouse, Baca survived for 33 hours before the Texans, having unloaded some 4,000 bullets into the shack, finally gave up and rode away. Today Reserve is the keystone of a cattle and timber industry on the southern fringe of the Apache National Forest.

About 150 sage-colored miles to the east is Magdalena. The central landmark is the scrubby yucca and cholla-covered hulk of Magdalena Mountain, also known as Magic Mountain. It became a refuge for miners in the old days when bands of marauding Apaches, believing it to be haunted, would give up the chase near this peak. Three miles up the hill is the ghost town of Kelly, now nearly buried beneath the juniper and pinyon. An old church survives and seems as much an ingredient of the natural beauty as the pine and cactus surrounding it, the steeple poised against the rapidly rising land and limitless sky.

Organ Mountains

Late afternoon on the New Mexico desert

City of Rocks State Park

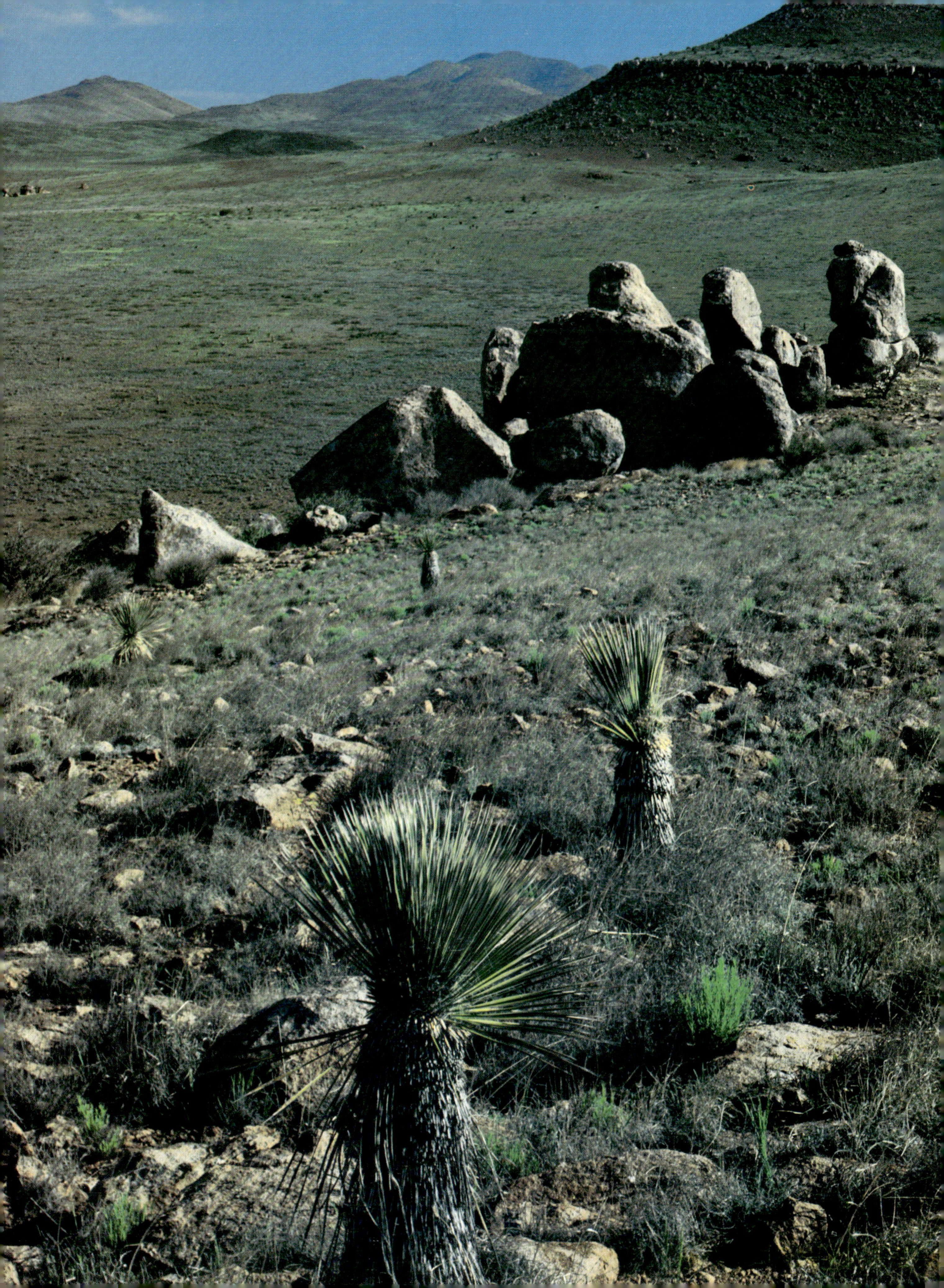

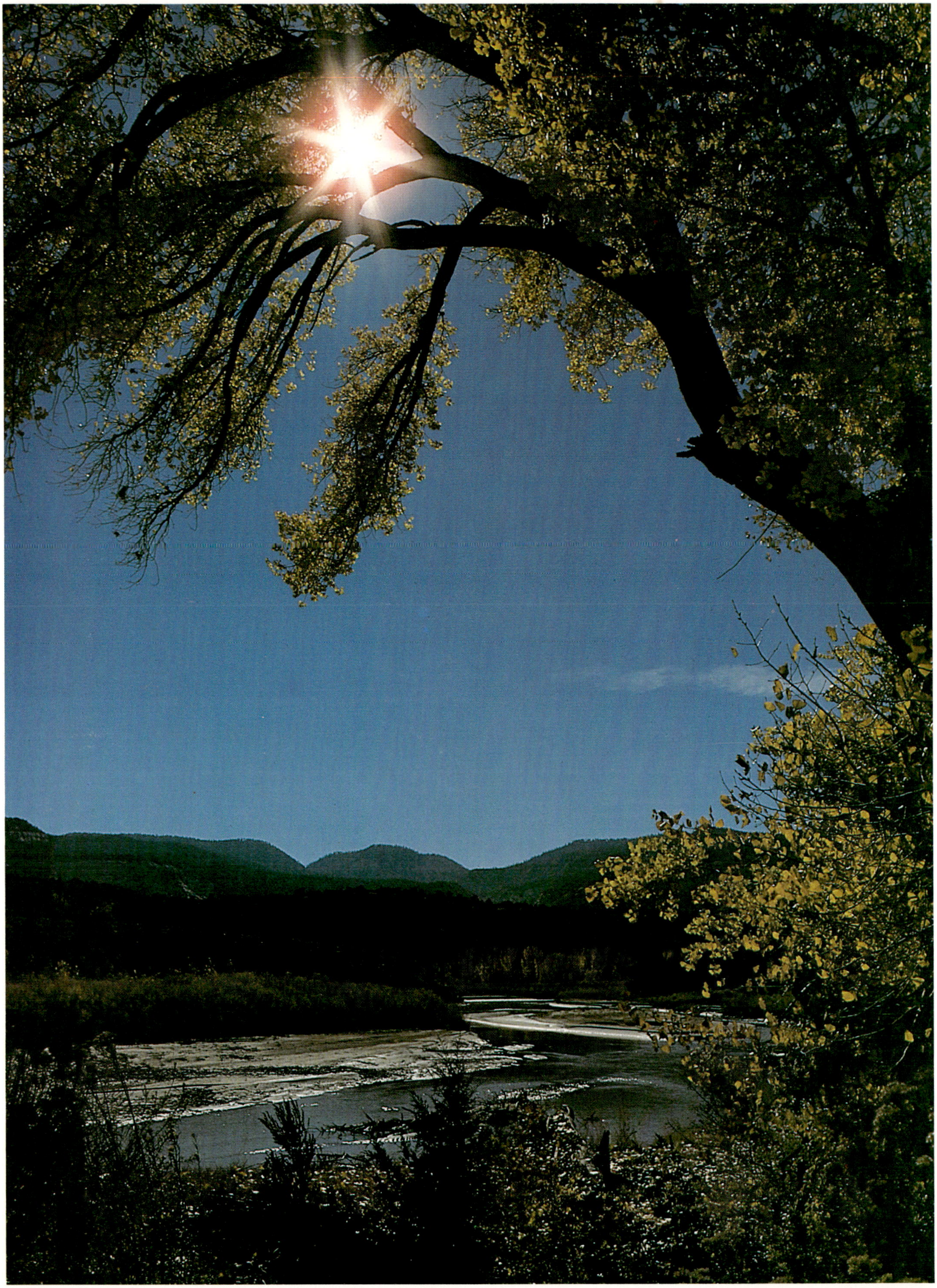

Electric Storm

Chama River, Santa Fe National Forest

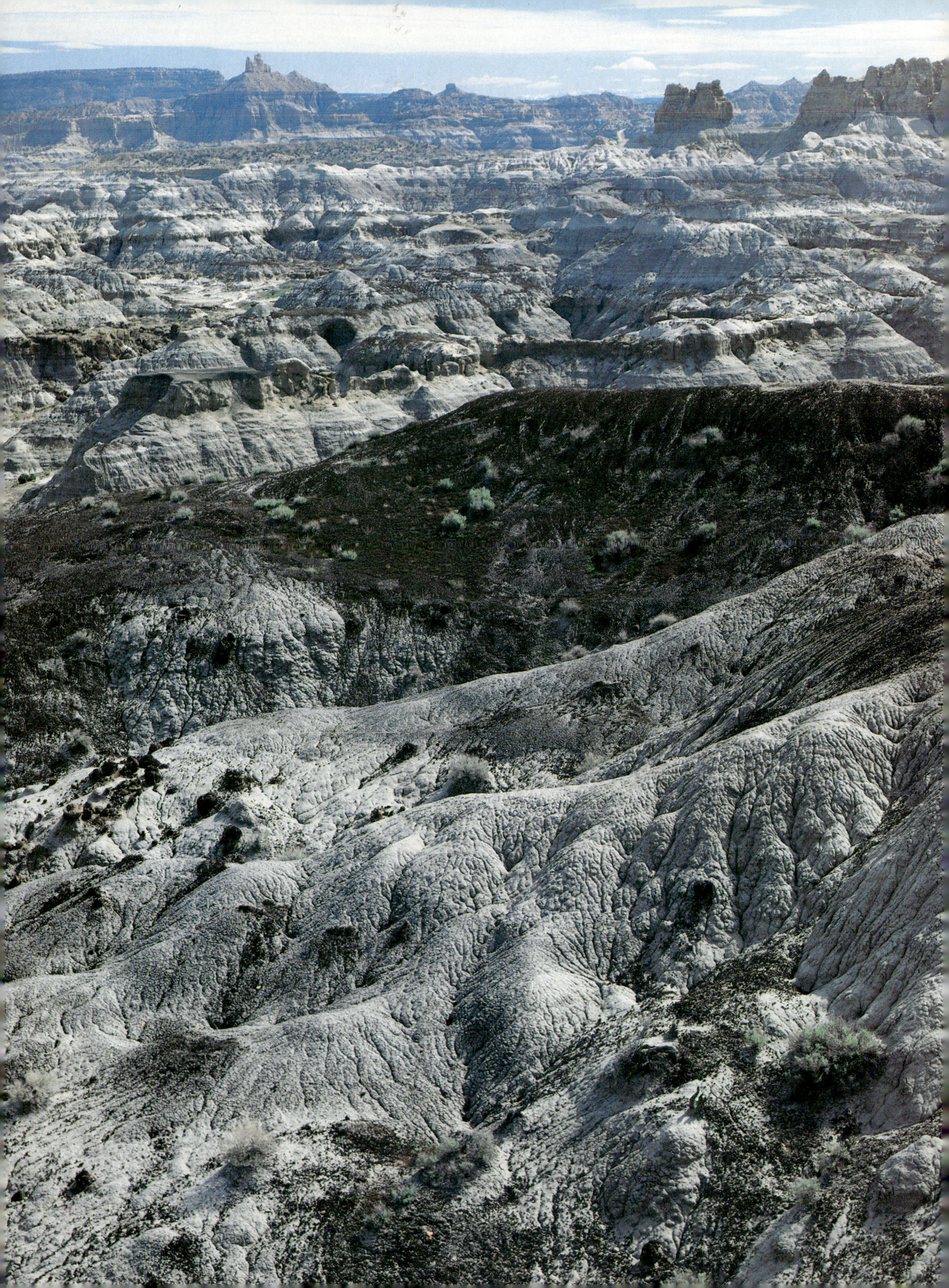

Jemez Mountain Range near Jemez Springs

Angel Peak Recreational Area

North-Central—
Pueblo Heartland and
the Historic Cradle

Albuquerque is an anomaly in New Mexico: a large, modern city. It's an unexpectedly handsome one, this metropolis that has mushroomed from a small Spanish trading post, sprawling in every direction on a plane of earth at the feet of the Sandia Mountains. The gleaming geometric grid of contemporary architecture beneath the string of peaks offers a study in contrast, but the real attraction is Old Town where the city was born. The flavor is distinctively Spanish with a romantically subdued gas-lit plaza, adobe houses, abundant wrought-iron work and a historic church where mass has been said every day since its founding in 1706.

The mountains on the outskirts of town are the biggest recreation spot around. The west face, seen from Albuquerque, is a plunging mass of Precambrian granite, while the eastern slopes are a gentler terrain of wooded limestone. Some of the state's best climbing and hiking trails can be found here and, for the dreamer, tales of an undiscovered fortune in gold coins buried somewhere in the foothills. The Sandia Peak Tramway, longest in the nation, carries you quickly to an elevation two miles above sea level and, assuming clear skies, renders a view that is incomparable. The entire mountainous North-Central region is visible: about 10,000 square miles of wonderfully diverse scenery.

In the mountains north of Albuquerque dwell the larger part of New Mexico's Pueblo Indian population. The Zia, Jemez, and San Felipe Pueblos occupy a large crescent of rugged country bordering the Santa Fe National Forest. The Pueblos are sedentary and artistic people, and their work is evident throughout the area: fine pottery, shell and turquoise jewelry, baskets woven of dried yucca leaves, and water-color paintings. The unique pueblo dwellings are the oldest "cities" in the United States. They vary in style and use, some located in the steep highlands and others on

Spring flowers on Organ Mountains

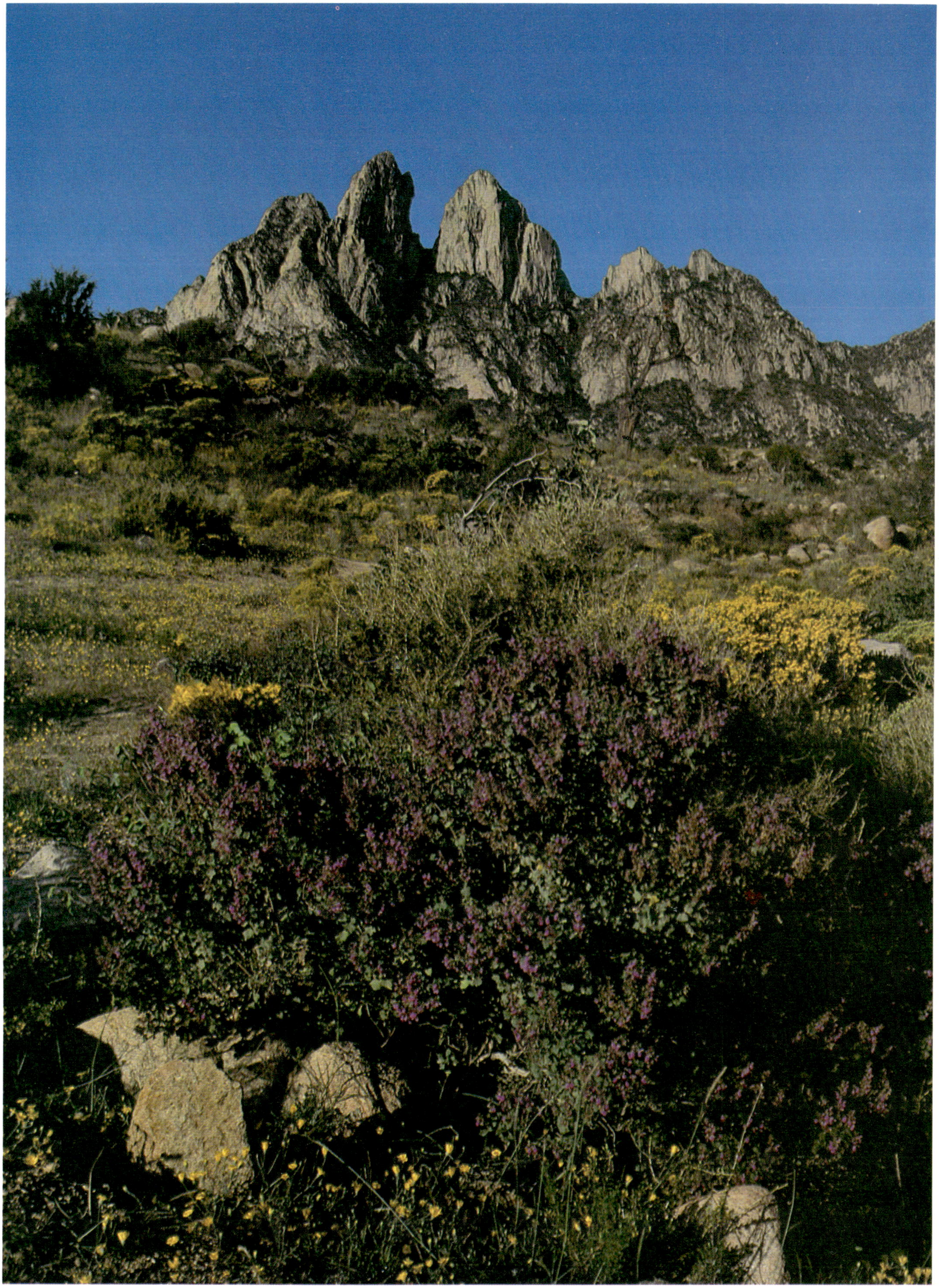

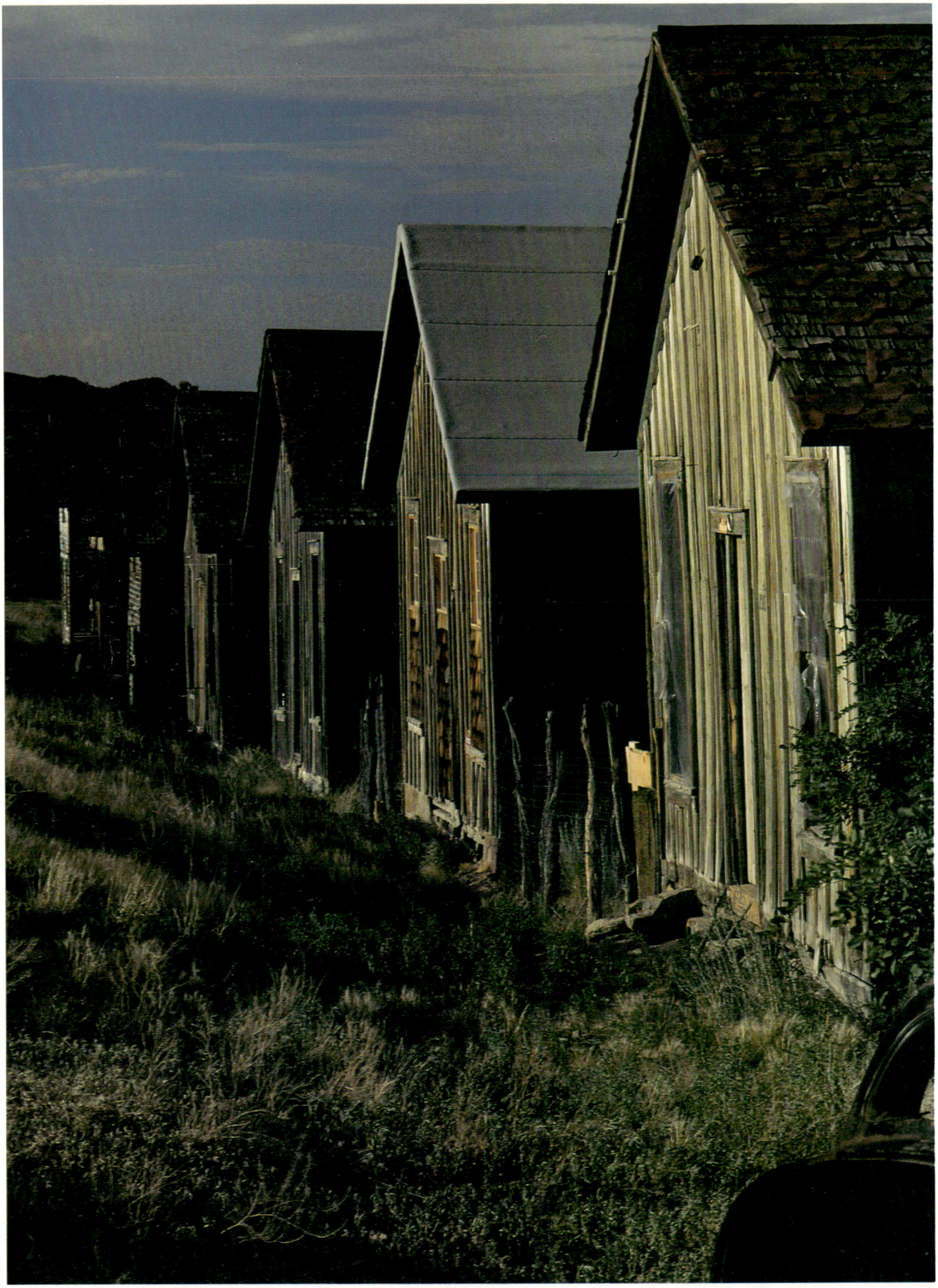

the more accessible valley floors. The Pueblo past is also on display here, most impressively at Bandelier National Monument and the Puye Ruins. These cliff dwellings, artifacts, and petroglyphs date from the large Pueblo population of 1200 to 1500 A.D.

The Jemez Mountains with their steep mesas and canyons are heavily forested and dotted with wildly eroded formations. This is good climbing country and if you know what you're doing, most of the summits are accessible. Santa Clara Peak at 11,561 feet is the giant of the range. But the primary feature here is the huge volcanic bowl or caldera, a collapsed valley surrounded on all sides by mountains. The caldera comprises 176 square miles of meadows and mesas funneling down to a bare, ancient lake bed.

On the edge of the caldera is the once-secret city of Los Alamos where the world's first atomic weapon was developed. Today the Los Alamos Scientific Laboratory, high in the stands of ponderosa pine, is an energy research lab where nuclear, solar, and geothermal energy sources are studied and tested. (A note about New Mexico energy: this is one of the country's biggest energy producing states. In addition to uranium, potash, low-sulphur coal and natural gas, New Mexico boasts a large-scale coal-gasification project. And much of this energy leaves the state to supply other less-endowed portions of the nation.)

North, past the San Pedro Mountains, is the mighty Rio Chama and its smattering of spectacular lakes. Following the river you are in the Brazos area where a 1,500 foot rock tower rises dramatically from the mouth of Brazos Box Canyon, and just four miles away, the stunning Brazos Peak.

To the east of the Jemez Range is the crown jewel of New Mexico's cities, Santa Fe. Located at the southern terminus of the Sangre de Cristo Range (the highest mountains in the state), Santa Fe is not only the capitol, but the historic and cultural center as well. Nicknamed "The City Different," Santa Fe is truly unlike any American city of the 20th century. Billboards, skyscrapers, and urban blight are nowhere to be seen, and in their place is a refreshing display of traditional Spanish architecture. The oldest public building in America is the Palace of Governors (1610) in central Santa Fe, while the current capitol building (The Roundhouse) is designed in the circular format of an Indian kiva. A short distance away, along the Santa Fe River, is the city's oldest church, dating from the mid-17th century, and an adobe structure which may very well be the oldest house in the United States.

Outside of town, wilderness recreation is within easy reach. The splendid Glorieta Mesa spreads southward and in the opposite direction, the Sangre de Cristos are full of ghost towns, ski resorts, Indian pueblos, forests of spruce and aspen and

Huge crevasse south of Taos

frosty mountain streams. The splendor of the Sangre de Cristos is perhaps most evident in the Taos area, 67 miles by road north of Santa Fe. People come to Taos for three reasons: the unparalleled ski slopes, the most prominent of New Mexico's art colonies, and the majestic serenity of this magic spot in the mountains. There is an indescribable, alluring charm to Taos that seems to draw certain souls like a magnet. There are scores of inhabitants who came to visit years ago and somehow never quite got around to leaving. When the English novelist D.H. Lawrence came here, he proclaimed Taos the most beautiful spot on earth, and to take in the view from the still-standing Lawrence ranch is to understand precisely what he meant.

These majestic mountains are the Taos Range, a sub-range of the Sangre de Cristos. A good way to see them is to take the circular route of state roads which loop through the Carson National Forest and back around to Taos. This is one of the most beautiful drives available in New Mexico, or anywhere for that matter. Red River Pass cuts through the mountains and provides a path to Eagle Nest Lake. There are views of the Cimarron country to the east, and, a few miles from the lake, the towering summit of Wheeler Peak, the highest mountain in New Mexico, measuring 13,161 feet. The road curls south at this point and completes the circle around the Pueblo de Taos Indian Reservation.

The Taos Range in some respects is the epitome of the beauty that is New Mexico. Nowhere else are the glories of an untamed nature so evident and so striking. The multiplicity of peaks and gorges, the forests transformed only by the steady march of seasons, the marvelous ski bowls and alpine lakes may find the traveller a trifle distracted with plans of a return trip. On the other hand, it's entirely possible that he may plant his boots and decide like those before him (Indian, Spaniard, and Anglo alike) that he can't, just now, think of any sensible reason ever to leave.

(Following page) Taos Range, Sangre de Cristo Mountains